Modernism has only one rule: to constantly create, invent, and reshape using the latest modern technology and science. Modernism has **no limits.**—*Valerie Pasquiou* • Modernism is difficult to define because it's not one **definitive style.** It can be both minimal and baroque, rectilinear and curvilinear, monochromatic and **colorful.**—*Fern Simon.* • The number one way to make an interior modern is to have **spaces flow** into each other.—*Benjamin Noriega-Ortiz* • What is truly modern is to create something ahead of the moment that then stands as **timeless.**—*Kara Mann* • Modernism is a **perfect response** to our hectic, loud, and chaotic contemporary life. People want and need **calm,** sustainable, and rejuvenating environments.—*Roger Faulds White* • Color is the key to making modern design warm and **accessible.**—*Marjorie Skouras* • Modern is not cold per se; it can have texture and age through the honest use of **ageless** materials like stone, brick, and plaster. **White** is definitely not a requirement.—*Ted Flato* • Modern design doesn't have a particular color, but there are colors that are **uniquely** modern: fire-engine red, cobalt blue, canary yellow, etc.—*Carlos Martinez* • Even in a modern environment, if you don't involve all the senses, it is hard to **convey emotion.**—*William Sawaya* • Sometimes less without more is just less. "Empty" should not be a design **statement.**—*Kelly Monnahan* • Anything can be modern depending on the context. An overstuffed sofa covered in floral chintz can look modern if it's plunked down in a raw **industrial** loft. Modern is about **unexpected** juxtapositions.—*Jonathan Adler* • The key to mixing the antique with the modern is the **quality** of the individual pieces, the way they work with the architecture, and **restraint.**—*Anthony Baratta* • If Louis XIV lived today, do you think he would build Versailles the way it is, or would he call in some **starchitect** to build it?—*William Sawaya* • Modernism at its best can have a **meditative** effect on our hectic lives. It has the capacity to connect us with nature, and nature has the capacity to connect us with our better selves.—*Max Levy* • Modernism is about **editing,** editing, editing.—*Doug Meyer*

Design 100

First published in 2010 in the
United States of America by
Filipacchi Publishing
1633 Broadway
New York, NY 10019

Metropolitan Home is a registered trademark of Hachette Filipacchi Media U.S., Inc.

Design: D'Mello+Felmus Design Inc. (www.dmellofelmus.com)
Editor: Julie Gray
Manufacturing: Lynn Scaglione and Annie Andres

ISBN-13: 978-1-933231-99-0
Library of Congress Control Number: 2010921542

Printed in China

Metropolitan Home®

Design 100

The Last Word on Modern Interiors

By Michael Lassell

Photographs produced by Linda O'Keeffe, Creative Director, and the editors of *Metropolitan Home*

By Way of Introduction

Welcome to *Design 100: The Last Word on Modern Interiors*. In a real sense, this book has been in the works for 20 years, since the first "Design 100" issue of *Metropolitan Home* was published. The D100, as it came to be called, was conceived by *Met Home*'s editorial staff as 1989 was turning into 1990. It was meant to be a survey of the best in the world of home design, including gardening and food, which were regularly covered in each monthly issue. "Design" was given the broadest possible definition.

The first D100 list included architects and their buildings, interior designers and their rooms, high-end and affordable sofas and chairs, tableware, kitchen gadgets, even not-for-profit organizations that were using good design to help make a positive difference in the world. The point of the exercise was to report on the direction of modernism, to celebrate its achievements, to expand its boundaries, and to win friends and influence people with contemporary sensibilities.

Happily, that experimental issue was an immediate hit with our readers and the design community. We celebrated the list with a party, which was like a big family reunion. Some recipients traveled great distances to attend, as being included on the list carried real industry cachet, which was extremely gratifying.

In the beginning, the D100 was published periodically, about every other year. As the world of modern design began to expand, however, so did the frequency of our tribute to the movers and shakers who embraced modernism to improve the aesthetics and the quality of our daily lives. Eventually, we started producing a D100 issue annually, constantly broadening our definition and throwing our net wider, conscripting scores of FOTMs (Friends of the Magazine) all over the country to scout locally and make nominations.

The last D100 issue of *Met Home* was published in June 2009. The cover lines read "Our Favorite People, Places & Things," plus "The 5 Best Homes in America," which may have been the tiniest bit of an exaggeration—or may just have been an expression of our great enthusiasm for the contents. The issue included an elegantly refined California home designed by Barbara Barry, a great cabin in the woods by Seattle architect Tom Kundig, a sleek condo conversion in Chicago, a "green and simple" summer place in upstate New York, and a madly colorful and edgily eclectic Florida house inhabited by Miami-based designer Doug Meyer.

In that issue we offered our imprimatur to architects Renzo Piano, David Rockwell, and Jeanne Gang, and and tipped our editorial hat to the Oslo Opera House and the new Acropolis Museum in Athens. Furniture choices included Tord Boontje's stool for Swarovski, Franco Albini's table for Cassina, and Darryl Carter's bench for Thomasville. We also heartily approved of the Droog store in New York City, lighting designer Hervé Descottes, chef Barbara Lynch, the Honda Insight, John Pawson cookware, the move to "green" Times Square, the newly discovered pink iguana of the Galapagos Islands and Rosangel tequila. Well, you get the idea.

Sadly, *Metropolitan Home* was permanently shuttered in November 2009, a casualty of a deeply wounded American economy and the rapidly shrinking world of print journalism. Even as we editors were packing our desks, however, we hatched a plan, and this book is it. We had already been discussing ideas for a new *Met Home* book to follow our enormously successful *Glamour: Making It Modern*, now in its fourth printing. The new book, which would be shepherded by Dorothée Walliser of Filipacchi Publishing (as *Glamour* had been), would be a kind of D100, but we would restrict it to interior design and architecture, which we thought would have the broadest appeal and the longest shelf life.

We wanted to give our faithful fans a farewell gift—after all, leaving the party without saying a proper thank-you and good-bye is just not polite. But we wanted to produce a book that was more than just a valediction. We wanted *Design 100* to be a working sourcebook of great ideas for home design, even for people who had never read an issue of *Met Home*. We hoped to inspire creativity in fashioning personalized living spaces that would be infused by the energy of the D100 issues of the magazine. And we took the opportunity to print some of the many great projects we had already photographed but not yet gotten onto the newsstand.

Three veterans of *Met Home*'s art staff signed on to work on the book project: former design director Keith D'Mello, his deputy art director, Jeff Felmus, and photo editor Cathryne Czubek. As the writer, I made a preliminary selection of about 200 locations, both whole residences and single rooms—trying for a mix of houses and apartments, of highest-end mansions and accessible family homes, of geography (both U.S. and abroad), and of designer experience, opening the door to veterans and newcomers alike.

Five of us winnowed the 200 down to the 100 you see here, based solely on aesthetics. Almost miraculously, the lively mix I had hoped to achieve in the original selection survived the final cut. (The final choices, it must be confessed, exhibit a certain reasonable prejudice on behalf of locations that had not already appeared in *Glamour* and previous *Met Home* books.)

The 100 places represent the work of well over 100 designers and architects, since many projects had several of each. An additional 100 individuals worked on the original stories as writers, photographers, and producing editors. So, a lot of talent has gone into this book, which we are proud to have represent the best of the best of *Met Home*'s 30-year history (which doesn't even include our years before that, as *Apartment Life*).

It would have been nice to publish even more photographs of every location, but that would have meant really tiny pictures (which has never been the *Met Home* way) or a book the size of an encyclopedia. So, sometimes one picture has to speak volumes. In our electronic world, however, more images are as close as the nearest computer, since almost all of the architects and designers who appear in the book have websites. Many of these sites have additional photographs of the projects printed here. And all of those Web addresses are provided in the resources and credits at the back of the book.

Each of our locations was laid out individually. The order in which they appear is one that makes sense visually. It does *not* represent a hierarchy of "bestness." No. 1 isn't the best; no. 27 isn't "bester" than no. 78. The 100-word paragraphs that accompany each of the homes are contrived to offer some explanation of just what it was that appealed to us. The citations themselves (like "The Best Bathroom in Britain") describe the spirit of the choices, but they are a bit tongue-in-cheek: There were no actual categories guiding our final choices. However, each of the 100 represents some key theme of *Met Home*'s editorial coverage.

As with *Glamour*, we enlisted the aid of the architects and designers in providing some collateral text for the book in the quotations that appear on the end pages (inside the front and back covers) and on some of the stories. These remarks, which only sometimes accompany the work of the individual quoted, are an attempt to help define "modernism" and/or what is "modern" in the world of design. This is no mean task, since the word is used interchangeably to denote a period of classic avant-garde design as well as the work of people currently engaged in its restless evolution.

In closing, I would like to thank my hardworking collaborators on this book. I dedicate it to everyone I have worked with at *Met Home* over the years, including "my" phenomenal writers, but especially to the last editorial staff standing when our wonderful magazine closed its doors forever: Donna Warner (editor in chief), Keith D'Mello (design director), Lisa Higgins (executive editor), Linda O'Keeffe (creative director), Arlene Hirst (deputy director, design and news), Jeffrey Felmus (deputy art director), Susan Tyree Victoria (senior editor, design and architecture), Cathryne Czubek (photo editor), Katherine E. Nelson (senior market editor), Jessica Mischner (associate articles editor), Rachel Lexier (assistant design and architecture editor), Lenora Jane Estes (assistant articles editor), Callie Jenschke (digital editor), Courtney Woods (assistant to the editor in chief), Natali Suasnavas (art assistant), and Julie Gray (copy editor, who has returned to have her way with the text of *Design 100*). Thank you for everything. You've all done very well!

Michael Lassell
Features Director, *Metropolitan Home*
New York City, 2010

Most Striking (and Surprising) Fireplace
Toronto, Ontario, Canada

For her own home in Canada's largest city, designer Elaine Cecconi, of Cecconi Simone, created this minimalist dining room, outfitted with rift-cut oak furniture designed by her firm and gossamer *Random* light fixtures by Bertjan Pot for Moooi. But the room's outstanding feature is an extraordinary one-off open fireplace, which is made, somewhat astonishingly, from fluted black Corian, the popular countertop composite that has found new life in an infinite variety of home applications. Cecconi also designed her kitchen cabinets of Corian and used it to camouflage all her appliances, applying the material to her refrigerator, dishwasher, etc. For a dose of tradition, her countertops are Corian, too.

2

Most Singular Penthouse on the Upper West Side
New York City

When a forward-thinking young couple bought this penthouse, they called in design guru Jonathan Adler to create a comfortable and playfully glamorous home. Aiming for "hotel-ish opulence and squishiness," Adler tried to make the new place look as though it had been around for a while, but not in a traditional way. In the living room, vintage lamps cast their light on custom furniture; the entryway has a wall of tiles glazed in actual platinum; and the dressing room features a Madeline Weinrib hassock. Now it's a great place for a party or a quiet evening in—and there's no other place remotely like it.　⋯⟩

Ornamentation is a means of communication. It provides dimension, texture, pattern, depth, and spirit. It livens up space to create complementary conditions, to move the eye, to give richness to surfaces, materials, and objects. —*Karim Rashid*

3

Best Home Kitchen for a Professional Chef
Purchase, New York

Pino Luongo has been cooking in Manhattan since he arrived from Tuscany in 1981, having opened 16 restaurants since. For his home, north of the city, he wanted a sleek modern kitchen to match the Milanese modern interiors of the other rooms. He turned to Bulthaup, the premium German kitchen manufacturer, whose designer, Feroza Jonuschat, specified aluminum and dark-oak veneer under-counter cabinetry, open shelving, and a 112-inch-long island to go with professional-grade appliances. Fit for a master chef, this is also a family kitchen, where the maestro, his wife, and their three children frequently cook together, singing Italian pop tunes while they stir.

Best Balanced Room for a Well-Balanced Meal
Washington, D.C.

The tasty dining room that designer Lori Graham created in a freshly renovated 1912 Kalorama neighborhood home is a perfect invocation of Janus, the two-headed Roman god of doorways, who looks forward and back at the same time. Graham's appetizing choices include a subdued Oushak carpet, antique chairs decorated with horn, and a contemporary *Rossini* table from Armani/Casa. The fireplace surround is vintage limestone (from Chesney's), but Graham designed the mirror herself; and the photographs are from Donald Sultan's decidedly modern "Smoke Signal" series. (It's a shame the U.S. Congress can't manage this kind of cooperation between seeming opposites.)

Most Meditative Master Suite
Los Angeles, California

When Canadian singer k.d. lang went looking for her first house, she fell for a heavily beamed, secluded place that had been built in 1940 and once served as the rustic hideaway of Rock Hudson. After six months in her unfurnished home, she called in Valerie Pasquiou and Constance Delorme to personalize it to her taste, which ran to Arts and Crafts designers Greene & Greene. The French-born designers went East-meets-West natural with comfort pieces mixed with Asian antiques. The bedroom features a custom teak bed and billowing gold silk curtains that softly catch daylight and canyon breezes.

Most Graphic Staircase (Pure and Simple)
Hollywood, California

Darryl Wilson grew up in Hollywood: His father was a builder, his uncle a designer whose clients included Cher (who used to babysit for Darryl). So when he saw this 1963 cliff-hanger (hidden under 40 years of inappropriate "modernization"), he wanted to turn it into "one of the coolest houses in Los Angeles." Which he did, with rare purity of form, starting in the foyer, which he upgraded with a dramatic poured, lightweight terrazzo staircase (each tread is a different shape) with a clean-lined, vaguely retro, blued-steel railing. The result is just perfect for an *haute* groovy entrance.

6

Brightest Idea for a Boys' Bath
Northern Iowa

E. B. Min and Jeffrey Day, partners in Min|Day, conveniently located in San Francisco and Omaha, created a captivating lakefront vacation home on the border of Iowa and Minnesota. The house itself is built from concrete and wood with lots of glass; the interiors have white walls with eye-catchingly colorful furniture. The bathrooms take color up a notch. The master is white, but another is lime green. The clients' three sons share this one—highly efficient, but unexpected. The Boyd "sconces" (with bulbs behind etched mirror) are set flush to the vanity wall; the cabinetry is covered with a laminate from the Italian company Abet. And no fighting over the sinks—each guy has his own.

8

**Best Reuse of
a Historic Structure**
Ontario, Canada

When a Toronto telecommunications executive and outdoorsman decided
to build a weekend home, he knew where to look: at land his grandfather had
bought in 1932 on a river northwest of the metropolis. The property included
a gristmill, built in 1857, that had been part of his boyhood summers. Architect
William E. Bennett, an expert in historic architecture, updated the mill (unused
since a hurricane wiped out the dam in 1954) without destroying its sublime
symmetry. For the interiors, David Powell and Fenwick Bonnell were charged
with finding an artful harmony between old and new. The result is classic. ⋯⋗

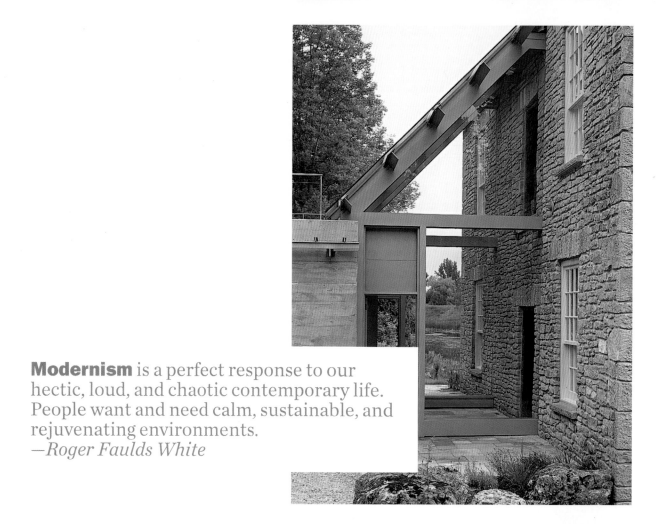

Modernism is a perfect response to our hectic, loud, and chaotic contemporary life. People want and need calm, sustainable, and rejuvenating environments.
—*Roger Faulds White*

Most Masterful Morphologist
New York City

Karim Rashid is not just a designer, not even "just" an industry, although he has a creative finger in every pie in the bakery: He's a showman who likes to surprise and delight. And he's doing what he can with his computer to keep the eye of the 21st century on the here and now. Having created just about everything, from furniture and rugs to lighting and household objects, Rashid is a "blobophile" with the energy of an avalanche. "People think every shape has been done before," he says, "but it hasn't." His own apartment's walls are white, but the furnishings (all his designs) are colorful, with as few straight lines as possible.

Best Use of Mini Mosaics
Los Angeles, California

Before architect Tim Andreas got his creative hands on it, this bathroom was a small, dark room with a single tiny window looking out at the view. The newly expanded room is sheathed in ¾-inch glass mosaic mini tiles from Brazil, in a deep underwater green that Andreas matched to the laminated wall of clothes cupboards and drawers. Because he wanted to furnish the bathroom and not merely equip it, Andreas designed a vanity that looks like a classic midcentury credenza and backed it up against a wall of translucent glass. The bathroom, livened with hits of chartreuse, now doubles as a dressing room/closet.

11

Best Little Kitchen in the Midwest
Chicago, Illinois

The Windy City has a cache of iconic buildings, none more famous than two black Mies van der Rohe towers overlooking Lake Michigan. When architect Carlos Martinez turned two adjoining one-bedroom apartments and a studio in the complex into a single rambling flat, he located a small but attractive and enormously efficient kitchen right in the middle, making it a convenient locus of social, as well as culinary, activity. Martinez designed the movable, below-counter walnut storage, and he kept things light with a translucent partition behind it (the guest bathroom is on the other side). For panoramic food preparation, the island faces a window wall with drop-dead downtown views.

Hottest Shot of Color in Miami
Miami, Florida

Something about sunshine seems to require color, and you can find most of them in artist/designer Doug Meyer's 1941 block-and-stucco suburban home, where the coprincipal (with his older brother) of Doug and Gene Meyer hangs his many hats. Take for example the dark-lilac Florida room, where Andy Warhol's 1962 *Marilyn* presides over a vintage sofa covered in an IKEA fabric and orange cube tables of Meyer's own design. The floor is covered in a Gene Meyer rug; the giant tooth is Wendell Castle's *Molar* chair. The witty and winning room occupies a fun-seeking style slot midway between kitschy quaint and *you've got to be kidding!*

13

Best Modern Makeover
of a Historic House
Bucks County, Pennsylvania

Richard Ferretti and James Gager, two high-profile Manhattan art directors, had their sights set on an early 19th-century stone country house, so when they found this one, in a somewhat less-than-pristine state, their design minds started running overtime. They bulldozed an aluminum-sided addition from the 1940s, replacing it with a new structure that follows the roofline of the original house; then they added a modern fireplace with a chimney that seems as old as the local hills. They kept the interiors minimal, exposing the field-stone in every room and allowing the natural materials to serve as the art. ...⁝⟩

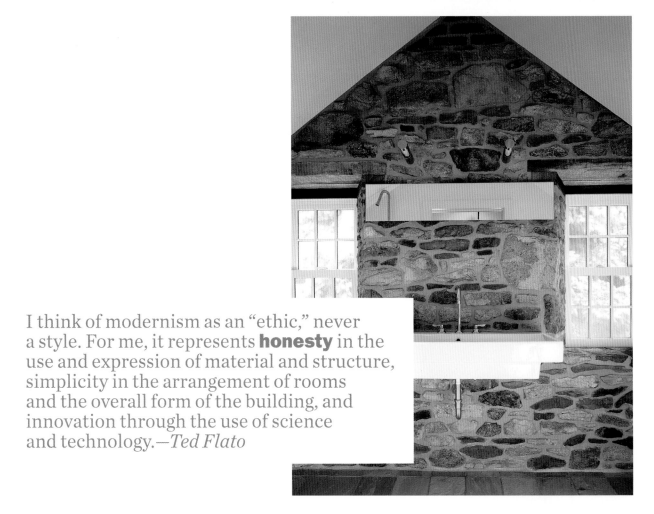

I think of modernism as an "ethic," never a style. For me, it represents **honesty** in the use and expression of material and structure, simplicity in the arrangement of rooms and the overall form of the building, and innovation through the use of science and technology.—*Ted Flato*

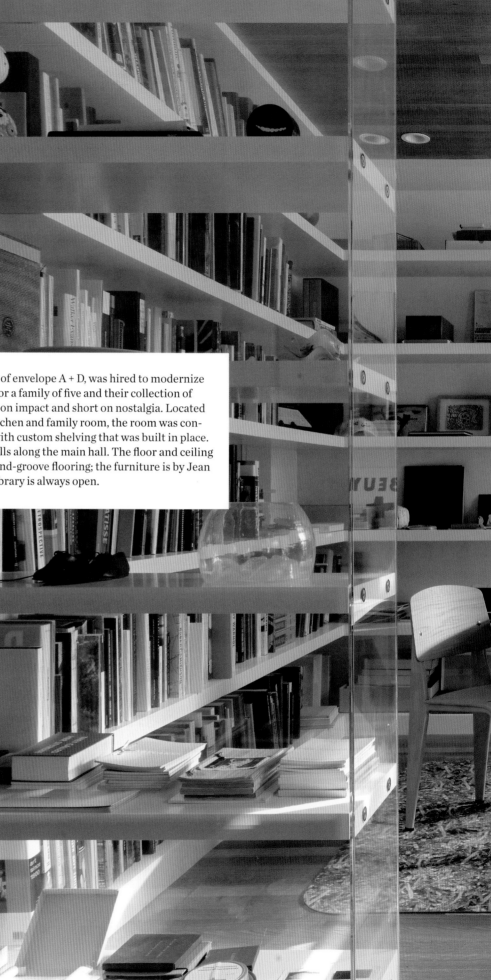

14

Best Reason to Study Art
San Francisco, California

When architect Douglas Burnham, of envelope A + D, was hired to modernize a 1930s house in Presidio Heights for a family of five and their collection of art, he created a library that is long on impact and short on nostalgia. Located on the first floor, adjacent to the kitchen and family room, the room was conceived as a "container" for books, with custom shelving that was built in place. Two glass "vitrines" stand in for walls along the main hall. The floor and ceiling are both quartersawn oak tongue-and-groove flooring; the furniture is by Jean Prouvé (from Vitra). Clearly, this library is always open.

Best Backyard Drive-in
Rural Pennsylvania

Designer, photographer, writer, TV personality, and latter-day Renaissance man Todd Oldham and his equally creative partner, Tony Longoria, share a country place on 14 acres of wooded land— and they make the most of their life in the great outdoors. They built a little gazebo that turns on a lazy Susan so they can catch the rays or the shade by rotating the whole room. And they added a deck washed in a verdigris stain that serves as an alfresco cinema after dark, adding as much mood-elevating color as possible with the comfy furniture, giving new meaning to "wait until dark." Popcorn, anyone?

16

Most Haute Couture Bedroom
New York City

China-born fashion designer Vivienne Tam, who was raised in British-dominated Hong Kong, is known for soft and colorful East-meets-West clothing that plays with ideas of "exotic" Asia. In her own Manhattan apartment (circa 1994), Tam draped an iron four-poster with mosquito netting and dressed it with a textural cotton cover over deeply fringed antique embroidered silk sateen from Beijing. Then she accessorized with Asian, African, and European antiques (including the English Victorian trunk used as a nightstand). The romantic result, said the late Richard Martin (resident fashionista of the Metropolitan Museum of Art), is "an idealistic globalism" (the very best kind).

17

Best Renovated Ranch
Los Angeles, California

The TV writer/producer who bought this 1953 courtyard ranch loves such California modernists as Rudolph Schindler and Richard Neutra, which was architect Steven Shortridge's cue to remove half a century's dubious redecoration and to open the place up (the master bath, at right, is open to the bedroom past a two-sided fireplace). Interior designer Carole Katleman brought in contemporary and vintage pieces like a pair of Gio Ponti armchairs, a Billy Haines sofa, and bronze chinoiserie chairs to sit on the new bamboo floors. Shortridge revealed the central steel ceiling beam as part of his totally satisfying keep-it-real approach that marries the natural with the manufactured.

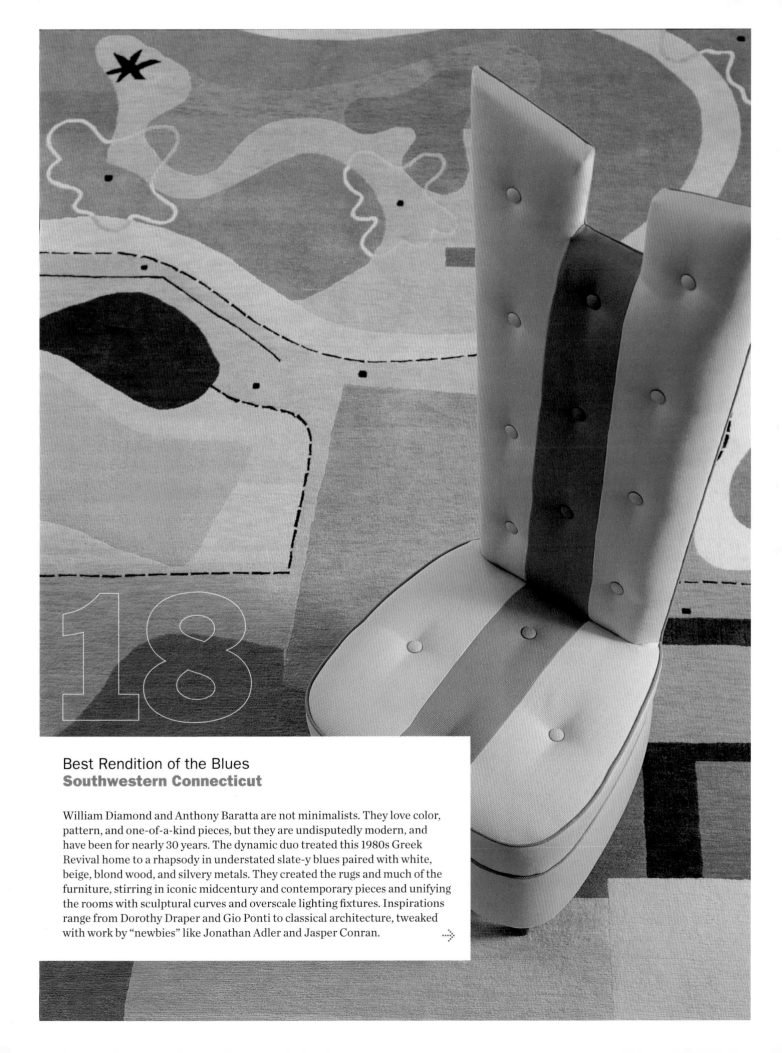

Best Rendition of the Blues
Southwestern Connecticut

William Diamond and Anthony Baratta are not minimalists. They love color, pattern, and one-of-a-kind pieces, but they are undisputedly modern, and have been for nearly 30 years. The dynamic duo treated this 1980s Greek Revival home to a rhapsody in understated slate-y blues paired with white, beige, blond wood, and silvery metals. They created the rugs and much of the furniture, stirring in iconic midcentury and contemporary pieces and unifying the rooms with sculptural curves and overscale lighting fixtures. Inspirations range from Dorothy Draper and Gio Ponti to classical architecture, tweaked with work by "newbies" like Jonathan Adler and Jasper Conran. ⋯⋯⟶

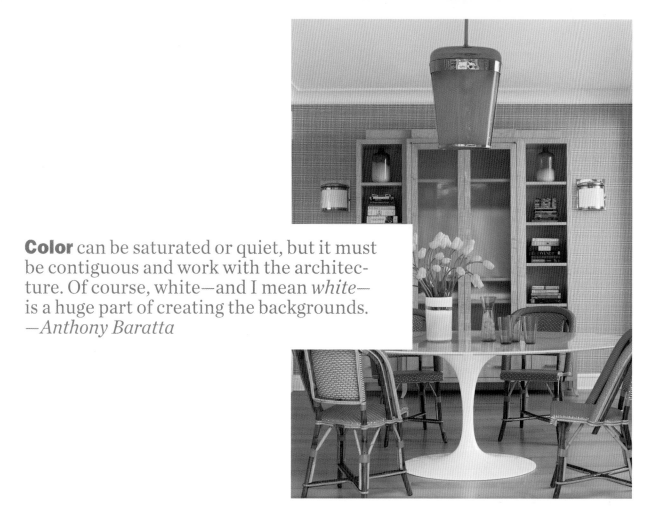

Color can be saturated or quiet, but it must be contiguous and work with the architecture. Of course, white—and I mean *white*— is a huge part of creating the backgrounds. —*Anthony Baratta*

19

Best Glass House Restoration
New Canaan, Connecticut

In 1958—the same year he designed Park Avenue's world-renowned Seagram Building in collaboration with Mies van der Rohe—Philip Johnson created this tranquil beauty not far from his own Glass House of 1949. In the closing years of the 20th century, new owners bought the place, hoping to restore some of the purity of "less is more" after years of neglect and alterations that couldn't have been "more" inappropriate. They turned to the nonagenarian Johnson himself to supervise the purifying resurrection, a labor of love that yielded deeply satisfying results worthy of preservation. As floor plans go, you can't get much more open than this. It's not a place to throw stones.

20

Most Intense Take on a Moroccan Rainbow
Tucson, Arizona

When designer Ronald Bricke's New York publishing client suggested a Moroccan palette for her Arizona getaway, he couldn't have been more delighted, having been impressed by the brilliant colors he saw on his own visits to the North African nation. Bricke's explosive visual feast begins in the foyer and continues in the living and dining rooms, all of which share a "fireworks in the spice market" aesthetic tempered by cool Mediterranean purples and blues. It's about as far from the anonymous neutrals of midtown Manhattan as you can go on the color chart, which is just what the vacationing client had in mind.

Most Photogenic Foyer
Chicago, Illinois

When you own one of the most significant private collections of photography in the country, you want to show it off. Artist Ellen Sandor and her husband did just that by turning the entrance of their vintage duplex into a picture-perfect gallery. Giving the lie to hanging everything at eye level, the couple grouped the works by subject, adding some non-photographic objects, like Marcel Duchamp's red and white license plate, a Plains Indian garment, and a rifle that was once owned by General George Custer. The welcome is perfect, but how do you persuade your guests to move into the living room?

Best Major Makeover with a View of Beverly Hills
Los Angeles, California

Vidal Sassoon's blunt-cut geometric haircuts helped define the 1960s, so when the master of haute coiffeur and his wife, Ronnie, found their dream home in the early 1990s, they needed someone equally creative (and wise in the ways of Euclid) to rescue the 1963 Mies-inspired house from decades of stifling plush. Totah's two-year "cleanup" involved stripping the place down to its structure, installing onyx terrazzo floors, and expanding the kitchen and master suite. His own furniture, which draws on appealing parabolic curves, helps soften the house; and the pieces (many of them on wheels) are easy to move, for maximum flexibility. "It's an open loft," said Totah, "Hollywood style."

23

Best Milanese Modern Manse on Maui
Kuli, Hawaii

When a designing couple decided to build a new house on the vacant lot next door to their traditional Hawaiian home, they called in the late great Ettore Sottsass, a design genius known for game-changing industrial products, post-Cubist ceramics, and the Memphis furniture movement. He based Casa Maui, only his second house in the U.S., on a table (the black horizontal is the top), arranging the rooms around it like a colorful pile of children's blocks. The interior is wide open, with meticulously customized spaces spilling into one another and into the surrounding countryside. What can you say, but *"Mahalo, maestro!"*

People live with way too much clutter. Modern spaces give us the opportunity to edit our environment down to only the most necessary things. —*Kelly Monnahan*

24

Best Remodel of an Urban Victorian
Chicago, Illinois

The owners of this turn-of-the-century home had a clear vision: Something that referred back to classic American farmhouses, but with a modern urbanity that spoke to today. They hired architect Peter Madimenos to expand, open up, and remodel the house in a crisply contemporary way, then turned to designer Kara Mann, after seeing her own apartment in an issue of *Metropolitan Home*. Mann worked her monochromatic magic on the interiors with layers of smoky, surprisingly dark neutrals, and selected premium furniture by the likes of Christian Liaigre and natural materials (the living room carpet is aloe fiber, the side table petrified wood). It's dramatic and domestic at the same time.

Sleekest Means of Moving On Up
San Antonio, Texas

The conversion of this 1926 redbrick candy factory had already begun
when the woman who now lives on the top two floors came looking for
a new place to live. She liked the concrete floors, walls of steel-framed
windows, and unlimited potential, so she bought the building and hired
architect Jim Poteet to transform the top tier for herself and her art collection. He called in frequent collaborator Patrick Ousey to help create
the ultimate multi-tiered white-on-white loft. The staircase between the
lower (living) floor and the upper (gallery) floor is a seamless, high-sheen
continuation of the floors and makes high drama from the purest of forms.

26

Most Awe-Inspiring Beach Palace
Miami Beach, Florida

In fashion and in home design, Gianni Versace managed to marry the Renaissance to rock and roll. When he set his heart on South Beach in the early 1990s, he thought big, buying an old apartment house and turning it into a pleasure dome for himself and his family (it really has a dome, complete with an observatory). He even knocked down the hotel next door to make room for a posh pool. When first published in 1995, Casa Casuarina (a step over the top from, say, Xanadu) was full of art, antiques, and Versace furniture—plus some spectacular mosaics. Sadly, Versace was killed outside this home in July 1997.

27

Most Tranquil Enclosure for a Japanese Soaking Tub
Whidbey Island, Washington

To build a small house a short ferry ride from Seattle, fashion designer Lynn Mizono hired Langley-based Carl Magnusson. The builder created an energetic, innovative 1,200-square-foot home that celebrates the natural environment of Puget Sound's most favored island. With its earth-based materials and neutral colors, it's a creative match for Mizono's clothing, which is architectural, loose fitting, and modern. The Japanese soaking tub is tucked behind the sink/vanity/mirror unit that faces the bedroom in an open plan. The meditative space is warmed by radiant heat in the floor. And the source of water for filling the tub? In the ceiling of course! This room is both now and Zen!

Timeliest Kitchen Collection
Miami, Florida

There are so many great midcentury clocks on the market these days—both vintage, retro, and reproduction—that it's nearly impossible to choose, so don't. This playful kitchen was designed by Glenn Heim during the renovation of a 1951 ranch house for a couple who love collecting: Their home proudly displays caches of Venini glass, Russel Wright aluminum, and Popeye ephemera. In the cheerful breakfast area, the clocks take the place of wallpaper or art. Not only is this a great way to display a collection, it's a lesson in the way that multiples work together as one. And no one is ever late for work.

29

Most Singular Home on the Coast
Malibu, California

Designer Kelly Wearstler is known as L.A.'s queen of "modern glamour," so when she and her husband bought a beach house with three other couples, she was given carte blanche to turn it into a comfortable, low-maintenance, kid-friendly, and unique getaway. Wearstler drew her palette from nature, with shapes and colors inspired by sand, beach stones, shells, and driftwood. She covered the floors with bleached walnut, throwing Bardiglio marble onto the walls and filling the place with overstuffed, oversize vintage and contemporary pieces, art furniture, and a collection of curios. And you can be sure the neighbors don't have one just like it, not even in trendy-sur-la-plage Malibu.

An emphasis on **craftsmanship** and natural materials—stone, wood, clay, iron—can warm up a space.—*Jonathan Adler*

30

Tastiest Dining Room in France
Les Arcs sur Argens, Provence

Architect Jean-Michel Wilmotte is known in France for poetic moderniza-tions of grand historic buildings. That made him a natural to remove several hundred years' worth of ill-thought alterations to the Château Sainte Roseline (named after Rossolina, a 14th-century mother superior of the abbey that once stood on the site, which is now a working vineyard). Perhaps the most dramatic space in the glorious renovation is this informal dining room, set in a barrel-vaulted wine cellar adjacent to the kitchen. Wilmotte designed the furniture and the see-through screen and added dramatic lighting that shows off African, Asian, and South American antiquities. What can we say, but *Bon appétit?*

Most Graphic Pop from a Can of Paint
Jackson, Mississippi

When John Lyle's brother and his sister-in-law asked him to modernize their 1970s ranch in the two brothers' hometown, the Manhattan-based designer decided to replace the standard suburban Southern decor with something more personal—and unusual. To release the home's inner diva, he based every room on a black-and-white palette but added a third, different color to each space. The sunroom was treated to a black floor and some super-graphic zebra stripes in homage to the '70s. The 1960s Russell Woodard aluminum chairs are vintage, but those new polka-dot cushions add a hot shot of mod moxie to what used to be an outdoor patio.

32

Best Bath with a View
Seattle, Washington

For his family's home on Queen Anne's Hill, architect Clint Pehrson created "a house that uses archetypal materials like metal, glass, concrete, wood, and stone in a straightforward but carefully crafted way." In the master bath, where walls are cinder block, he upped the materials ante, going way past "straightforward" to inspirationally gorgeous with glass mosaic tiles the color of lapis lazuli and a fireplace for long winter naps. This is a bathroom for meditation as well as ablutions, and—as enjoyable as the Space Needle cityscape is—the room is about the views inside as much as the world beyond the windows.

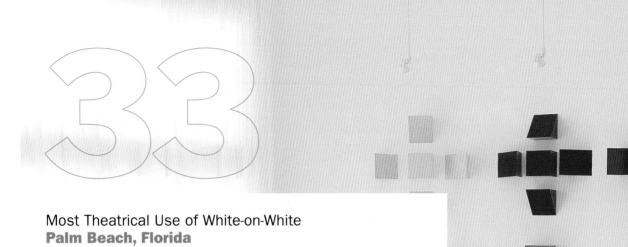

33

Most Theatrical Use of White-on-White
Palm Beach, Florida

They may be grandparents, but the couple who lives here are also minimalists.
They had to conform to the exterior "monotony code" of their vaguely Mediterranean community, but they called in designer Toby Zack to create something personal behind closed doors. Now the radically white interiors verge
on the space age, softened by furniture with curves, acres of sheer curtains,
and boldly colored art. It's practical too: Marble floors and a sofa covered in
outdoor fabric were chosen with active children in mind. Further mitigating a
possible feeling of sterility: witty juxtapositions and lots of views.

34

Best Modern Compound in the Wild
Buena Vista, Colorado

As a young kayaker, Ron Mason dreamed of a home on the Arkansas River. In 1973 he bought 17 pristine riverside acres, where he camped for three years in a Sioux-style tepee. In 1976 the architect (who started his career in the office of I. M. Pei) built the first structure, a modern log cabin, which was later followed by a guest cabin, and a "campanile" that adds a twist of Renaissance Italy to the local vernacular. Think of it as Tuscany Meets the Timberline. The simple shapes and natural materials of Mason's ongoing homage to the state's early gold-mining settlements will no doubt still look timeless in another hundred years. ⋯⋮⋗

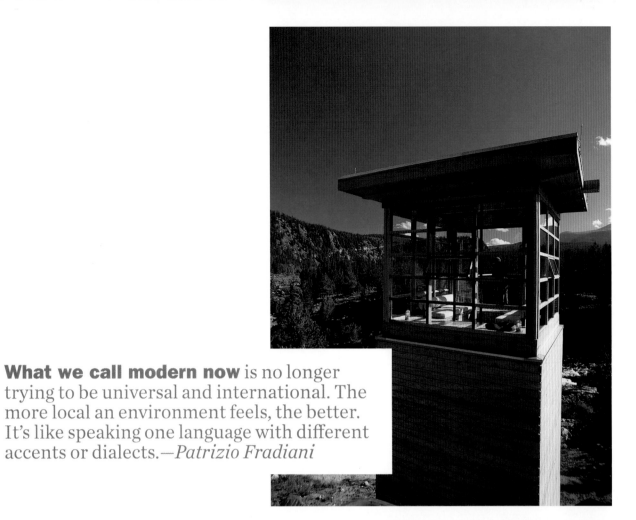

What we call modern now is no longer trying to be universal and international. The more local an environment feels, the better. It's like speaking one language with different accents or dialects.—*Patrizio Fradiani*

35

Best Abode in Beige-on-Beige
Los Angeles, California

Barbara Barry is one of the busiest interior designers working in America, yet everything about her rooms exudes calm, thanks in large part to the understated, neutral palette she's perfected over the years. For these clients, Barry gutted a West Side home and refinished and refurnished it in an urbane yet comfortable cross of *Father Knows Best* and the new modern mix—all the beiges unified by subtle undertones of gold and green. Much of the furniture is of Barry's design; the coffee table, however, is a vintage French piece from the 1950s, and the armchair at right is a 1929 *Bibendum* chair by Eileen Grey.

Best Repolishing of a Midcentury Jewel
Los Angeles, California

Academy Award–winning cinematographer Robert Richardson strives in his work, he says, to create "precision of line" and "the right balance of light and dark." The same two qualities guided the renovation of his 1952 Cliff May house, which is tucked away in a secluded canyon. Richardson enlisted the firm of Marmol Radziner to clean up the place, restoring it to May's original unfussy open-plan vision—well grounded and intimate with the wooded site. The design/build firm specified furniture, both vintage and contemporary, with lines as strong and subtle as the house's, all of which supports a natural ease, a certain timelessness, and an inviting equilibrium.

37

Most On Target Renovation of a Shotgun Cottage
New Orleans, Louisiana

If you fire a gun through the open front door of a shotgun cottage, they say, the bullet goes right out the back door. Shotguns were the simple homes of working people, but designer Ann Holden (of Holden & Dupuy) was aiming higher when she helped turn this abused turn-of-the-century Garden District house into an upscale three-bedroom home for a bachelor attorney. In the living room, where Lucite and glass meet puddled linen drapes and worn wooden antiques, a warm neutral paint color replaced mirrored green wallpaper; a gold Greek key border is a handsome stand-in for heavy crown molding.

38

Best Little Red Kitchen That Could
Brooksville, Maine

After raising eight children in Annapolis, Maryland, architect Chris Raphael and kitchen designer Peggy Wanamaker, who spend their spare time building homes with Habitat for Humanity, moved lock, stock, and design talent to a small town way up the East Coast. The new waterside home they built for themselves references traditional New England farm buildings but with a kick of modernism. They created this charmer of a kitchen, pairing saturated red walls and blond-wood cabinetry with countertops that used to be the marble walls of a bank. The open storage keeps the room fresh and clean, introducing the all-American farmhouse to a new millennium of warm cherry pie.

39

Best Second-Generation Renovation
New York City

Back in the late 1980s, this apartment was treated to a stem-to-stern renovation by design star John Saladino. Some 20 years and a fire in the building later, the Asian-born owner called on Benjamin Noriega-Ortiz (who had previously worked for Saladino) to spin his latter-day magic. The designer, known for his love of monochromatic environments and barely there fabrics, covered everything in pale neutrals and hung delicate, light-defusing Roman shades. Then he updated the mix with new pieces—including modern lounge chairs and a dining table with neoclassical roots—with accents of acrylic, crystal, silver leaf, and feathers. "Modern," Noriega-Ortiz insists, "doesn't have to mean hard."

Decoration and **ornamentation** are what make an interior human. People don't walk around naked—they decorate themselves. Why not decorate your rooms?
—*Benjamin Noriega-Ortiz*

40

Best Landscaped Roof
Bozeman, Montana

"Green roofs" in cities help cool buildings and convert carbon dioxide into life-sustaining oxygen, but settlers of the American West have had sod roofs for generations. This new house, by architects Dan Harding and Richard Charlesworth, is built right into a hillside, an ecologically smart solution. Landscape designer Linda Iverson used native plants and 'Covar' sheep fescue to cover the roof. The choices support her design philosophy, which is to leave the land as undisturbed by building as possible. Up on this roof, you're even closer to Montana's Big Sky—and it's engineered to catch water, to aid in conservation.

Freshest Take on the Blue-and-White Kitchen
Baltimore, Maryland

Architect Charles "Chip" Bohl and his wife, designer Barbara Bohl, tweaked the ever-popular blue-and-white kitchen palette when they moved into their downtown Baltimore triplex, choosing softer blues and warmer "whites" than traditional delftware and adding altogether modern touches, like the gleaming epoxy floor and the cutout between the kitchen and the adjacent master bedroom suite. To keep the eat-in cookery from being too slick, Chip designed a hefty table with a yellow Siena marble slab for a top and aligned it with an architectural take on a farmhouse sink made of Mexican limestone. Finally, a blue-and-white kitchen that doesn't look like a souvenir from Holland!

42

Best Balance of the Four Elements in a Single Room
Vancouver, British Columbia, Canada

When one of the owners of this new home dreamed up the design (literally), it fell to architect David Nicolay to translate that REM specter into reality for his clients, a couple who were jettisoning their separate pasts to start a new life together. Conceived as a simple glass box, the house was designed (per night vision) around a central fountain that splashes into a koi pond; with lots of visually receding glass walls to access light and views of the outdoors. The living room, which cozies up to the open-air fountain court, adds fire to the mix, as well as some classic pieces of furniture (and simpatico art by Darius Bebel).

43

Best Rooftop Playroom for Adults
New York City

Courtesy of architect Robert Siegel, the roof of this Manhattan penthouse is reached by a metal staircase with thick glass treads. Once on deck, guests may dine in the Brazilian îpe-wood pavilion at a custom precast concrete table that features a built-in ice "bucket" or lounge in a pergola with a transparent roof and a wall of running water. Or they can spiral up to the top of the metal-clad elevator shed and enjoy the hot tub or the driving range. It may not be accommodating in February, but for much of the year, this is the high life—city-style.

44

Most Relaxing House at the Beach
The Hamptons, New York

Designer Vicente Wolf is a poetic pragmatist. His rooms always feel modern, but he loves comfort and tranquility. He has a strong sense of history and a special affection for the decorative arts of Asia. For this house on Long Island, he not only worked his subtle magic in the choices of furniture, he showed a deft hand in visually enlarging the space, using horizontal mirrors in the living room and a storage wall in the kitchen that has glass doors on both sides. Like most Wolf projects, this one evokes a wow and a sigh at the same time. ⋯⋗

People who come to my home often ask me where I keep everything, the "stuff" of life. The key to living in a clean, modern environment is storage—**functional case pieces** and built-ins.—*Darryl Carter*

45

Wittiest Take on Bringing the Outdoors In
Los Angeles, California

When Marjorie Skouras was hired to design this classic neo-Spanish home from the 1920s, she didn't know just how outside the box her prominent clients would let her go. Having painted the living room a dazzling fuchsia, she ran with the ball when one of the homeowners suggested a bedroom that would be perfectly at home in Wonderland —or the local nursery. The four faux-boxwood topiary bushes were custom made by Janus et Cie; the headboard is a piece of art by Claudia Parducci. Drawing the line at Astroturf, Skouras specified forest-green carpeting as a softer alternative underfoot. Call it a re*tree*t.

Freshest Take on a Cozy Cottage
Cambridge, Massachusetts

Anything can be modern, even a 1920s worker's cottage in a college town with a history that predates the Revolutionary War. Husband-and-wife, Boston-based designers Jeffrey and Cheryl Katz chose a palette of muted blue, yellow, and green (looking from the dining room toward the living room, across the foyer/stairwell). Accessory colors were pulled from the living room's Tibetan carpet; new chairs are slipcovered in updated traditional fabrics like gingham and ticking (and all the furniture works in any of the rooms). White trim keeps it all as crisp as sheets dried in the sun. This place is a lesson in the power of paint!

47

Best Kitchen in a Glass Box
West Hollywood, California

When you can see the Pacific from your apartment—as you can from the 23rd floor of this landmark Sunset Boulevard building that abuts Beverly Hills—you want to see it as often as possible. So when her clients decided to downsize after their children were grown by moving up in the neighborhood, architect Alison Spear designed the new place, purchased from actor George Hamilton, with rooms you can look right through, including this incredible kitchen that occupies its own glass box (automatic gray-mesh screens can be lowered to hide clutter). Even the backsplash wall is glass, back-painted lavender.

115

48

Best Modern Casa South of the Border
Baja, Mexico

The Alaskan owners of this modernist home south of several borders were vacationing at the lower end of the Baja Peninsula when they fell in love—with the location. To create their sun-drenched dream, they turned to an old friend, architect Marsha Maytum, and her husband and business partner, William Leddy. Taking inspiration from the great Mexican modernist architect Luis Barragán, the designing couple created a series of interlocking indoor and outdoor spaces of concrete, stucco, and tile, reveling in sublime geometries and a hot, saturated palette that pops against the natural environment and frames ocean views. (P.S. As an added attraction, the house is entirely solar-powered.)

**Most Fashionable Makeover
of a Georgian Townhouse
London, England**

In the U.K., interior design doesn't get much more upper crust than the work of Kelly Hoppen. A creative force of nature, she's turned her own latest home, an 18th-century townhouse, into a venue for prodigious entertaining. The living room—with its glass fireplace wall, eclectic mix of furniture, and luxurious draperies of lingerie satin—occupies the entire second floor. The kitchen is right off the main entry and leads past a glass-enclosed cube that contains the appliances to a commodious dining room. The back garden is as much a play on comfort-meets-rationalist-symmetry as the welcoming interior.

Modern is all about function. The tricky question is, "What is the function?" My idea of the perfect functioning kitchen is probably not the same as everyone else's."
—*Kelly Monnahan*

50

Most Surprising
Cohabitation of Textures
Miami Beach, Florida

For an apartment high in the subtropical sky, architect Michael Wolfson (who trained under Zaha Hadid) found beauty in simple materials used in cool new ways. His Swiss clients asked for "sexy and modern." Wolfson thought "restrained, with luxurious textures." In the master bedroom, he floated a bed of his own design on a floor of fossil-preserving coral stone, contrasting the bronze bedspread with a straw "hula skirt" from Bed, Bath & Beyond (the texture of which is curiously in sync with Kate Bright's alpine painting). The plush drapes are real silk taffeta; the rock is faux (it's a Gufram piece from 1968).

Most Lustrous Salle à Manger
Chicago, Illinois

Designers Eric Ceputis and Harriet Robinson started with an unusual
North Shore house: Although the structure is new, it was built—by architect
Gregory Maire—to resemble a 1914 French manor-style home designed by
David Adler (itself informed by the Pavillon de la Lanterne built in 1787
at Versailles). So the designers went for French glamour, creating a dining
room that serves as the home's own Hall of Mirrors. The argent *chambre*
features furniture by Christian Liaigre and a phenomenal *Primitive* chandelier by Dennis & Leen. Iridescent window sheers softly filter the light,
which the silver-leaf wallpaper and mirrored console happily reflect.

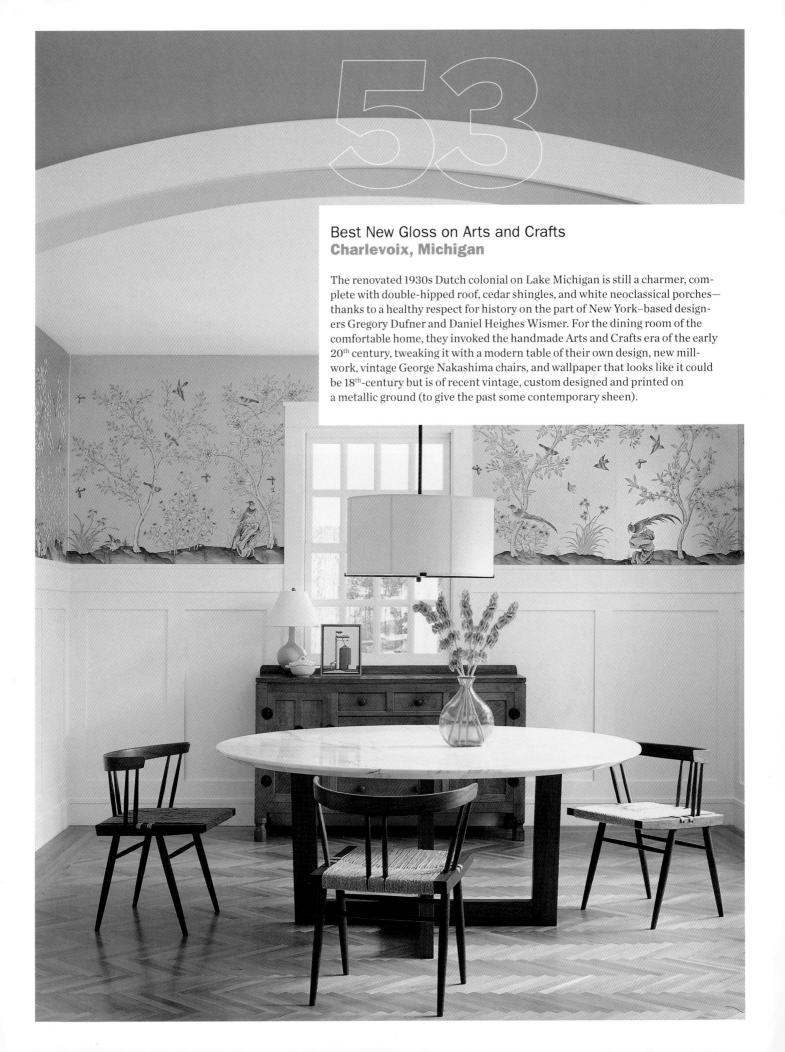

Best New Gloss on Arts and Crafts
Charlevoix, Michigan

The renovated 1930s Dutch colonial on Lake Michigan is still a charmer, complete with double-hipped roof, cedar shingles, and white neoclassical porches—thanks to a healthy respect for history on the part of New York–based designers Gregory Dufner and Daniel Heighes Wismer. For the dining room of the comfortable home, they invoked the handmade Arts and Crafts era of the early 20th century, tweaking it with a modern table of their own design, new millwork, vintage George Nakashima chairs, and wallpaper that looks like it could be 18th-century but is of recent vintage, custom designed and printed on a metallic ground (to give the past some contemporary sheen).

Best Boudoir for a Pop Diva
New York City

Twenty-five years ago, Madonna was channeling Jean Harlow and still speaking to her brother, interior designer Christopher Ciccone, so she hired him when she doubled the size of her duplex in a 1915 building overlooking Central Park. The gem in this "jewelry box," as he called it, was this saturated blue master bedroom with curvaceous white plaster moldings based on the stylized stage sets of Hollywood's Golden Age. The singular room manages to adroitly marry real glamour to a latter-day irony that's both astonishing and whimsical, with hints of Wedgwood as well as Alice on the far side of the looking glass.

Best Reinvention of a Major Modern Masterpiece
Phoenix, Arizona

By the mid 1990s, few of the original furnishings in the last home Frank Lloyd Wright designed still remained, and the place had been sadly abused. A new owner, who had long dreamed of living in this love letter to the circle, wanted to rethink the house, not restore it. She called in designer Mil Bodron, who upgraded materials, installed a pool, and moved in furniture by Wright, his contemporaries, and successors. At the client's suggestion, the new look embraces colors that were never part of the maestro's vision. The result is better than orthodox Wright; it is absolutely right—for a new place in time. ⋯⋗

Modernism is anything that Frank Lloyd Wright did. It is anything that Duke Ellington or Picasso did. These were artists who created new things where previously nothing existed.—*Charles Bohl*

56

Best Nearly All-White Kitchen Addition
Litchfield, Connecticut

This 1950s Cape Cod in one of New England's quaintest towns is, after two additions, the full-time home of a pair of energetic retirees, a fashion designer and a publishing creative director. Their first purchase for the expanded kitchen was the granite for the countertops, which they tied to the all-white theme of the house with a backsplash of Spanish tiles in a transitional beige. Now the creamy cookery not only provides a great place to prepare meals, but it offers a subtle light show, bringing out the contrast between white and beige in the morning while softening the differences as daylight fades in the afternoon.

Most Enthusiastic Spin of the Color Wheel
New York City

If you know the multilayered, extroverted fashions of designer Betsey Johnson, it should come as no surprise that her apartment is enveloped in her signature sunflower yellow—at least it was in 1997. "I have to be in bright color," she explains. "Yellow is uplifting, happy, and it changes drastically with the light." The walls are integrally colored plaster mixed with beeswax; the floor is a custom shade of paint she calls wisteria. Writer Michael Cunningham described the zany harmony of retro collectibles as a mix of Hindu shrine, Victoria and Albert Museum, and a good thrift shop. Sounds like Betsey, right down to her ruby slippers.

58

Best Interface of the Rustic and the Minimal
Hudson River Valley, New York

Architects Toby O'Rorke and Brian Messana didn't see any contradiction in giving their early-18th-century farmhouse a minimalist addition clad in oxidizing Cor-Ten steel. The unifying factor: geometric simplicity. The old building consisted of two rooms down and two up around a central fireplace; the addition, which has a limestone floor and a wall of glass overlooking the landscape, contains the kitchen and a guest room. The partners updated the fireplaces but preserved ceiling beams and plank floors; the split-timber table was made from a tree on the site. The house doesn't go *back* to nature, it goes forward.

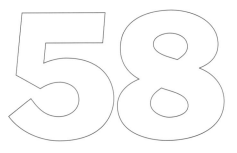

59

Best Transition from Outside to In
Los Angeles, California

When Scott Joyce was hired to remake this house in the Hollywood Hills, he decided to recast the entryway, formerly a gated courtyard open to the street. Working with "exterior designer" Tory Polone, Joyce closed off the view, making the uncovered front garden a more private place of transition. Now, amid lush new plantings, a small koi pond runs under a front step, and a glass wall marks the edge of the house proper. Interior designer Susan Young installed the chinoiserie screens. Arriving at the front door now gives guests the feeling that the home is unfolding, revealing more as they move through the house.

60

Best Modern Apartment with a Long Italian Past
Milan, Italy

William Sawaya, half of Milan's Sawaya & Moroni, one of the trendsetting city's most prestigious purveyors of cutting-edge furniture, lives in a classic 1920s apartment that came with a lot of antique decoration. He added even more, repairing the parquet and stained glass and restoring a mosaic entry floor. Then he filled the place with contemporary art and new pieces by creative colleagues like Zaha Hadid, Jean Nouvel, and Hani Rashid. Mixing periods, Sawaya believes, shows off personality and confidence. Much of the furniture, including the bed, bedroom chair, and dining table are Sawaya's own designs.   ⋯⋙

Antiques and vintage pieces make modern spaces look more credible and authentic. Conversely, modern designs also look great in a classical old house if you can achieve the right rapport with its proportions and ornaments.—*William Sawaya*

61

Best Bedroom with a Lake View
Horseshoe Bay, Texas

The home that Rick Archer designed for a neurosurgeon and his family sits beside (and partially in) a refreshing lake—an ideal retreat in the sun-baked days of a Texas summer. Archer manipulated the three stone and concrete living pavilions, which are connected by perimeter terraces and interior courtyards, to minimize the difference between indoors and out and to capture every passing breeze. Interior designer Emily Summers went soft but unfussy in complementing the rough walls and polished concrete floors. With a view like this, waking up is a daily pleasure, but leaving the bedroom is a problem.

Most Eccentrically Elegant Dining Room
Miami Beach, Florida

There probably isn't a style or period that designer Larry Laslo couldn't pull off with aplomb—he's that kind of designer—but given free rein, he'll likely be pushing the envelope. "I like to exaggerate scale," he says, leaving unsaid his penchant for exaggeration in general. Having first designed his edgy art-collecting clients' home in Colorado, he turned his talent to their winter condo, choosing a round Moura Starr table, attention-grabbing chairs by Christopher Guy (complete with his signature crisscross legs), and a hand-colored, cut-glass *18-Arm* chandelier from Miami's NIBA Home. In the process, he turned an open-plan dining space into an art installation all its own.

63

Best Renovation of
a Desert Classic
Palm Springs, California

The desert playground known as Palm Springs boasts an enormous supply
of midcentury American houses, and one of the best is a low-slung rambler
designed in 1963 by Donald Wexler for Dinah Shore—singer, TV personality,
and golfer—as a series of connected glass volumes. New (and creative) owners
called in designer D. Crosby Ross to collaborate on an update, which included
installing cedar ceilings, polished concrete floors, and an impressive selection of colorful contemporary furniture. He also blasted out the master bath,
replacing Dinah's old fur closet with a brand-new sauna, a very hot choice!

64

Best Compound Home
in the Lone-Star Vernacular
Kyle, Texas

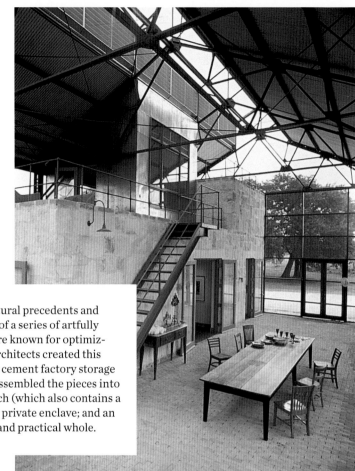

Noted for finding inspiration in industrial and agricultural precedents and for shaping green-conscious homes that often consist of a series of artfully connected mini buildings, David Lake and Ted Flato are known for optimizing the relationship between structure and site. The architects created this Hill Country home from a 180-foot-long, steel-framed cement factory storage "shed" being sold as scrap. Cutting it in three, they reassembled the pieces into side-by-side units: the world's largest screened-in porch (which also contains a stone-walled kitchen/living space); a corrugated-steel private enclave; and an open-air "carport," creating a harmonious, evocative, and practical whole.

Best Display of a Rare Cache of Collectibles
Seattle, Washington

Dale Chihuly—the undisputed world champion of glass art—no longer lives in his Seattle manufactory, a former boat-building shop on the shores of Lake Union, but he still maintains it as a homelike space. His own glass hangs over the 88-foot-long table (a single slab of fir) in a dining hall that used to be a roof deck (Eames chairs were salvaged from a school). In other rooms, he shows off Native American baskets (which have served him as a source of inspiration), Pendleton blankets, and art books without their covers. His accordions hang like Chinese lanterns from the ceiling, and more Chihuly glass lives in a lighted, enclosed trough in the pool. It's hard to imagine more loving or compelling display. ⋯⋯⃕

Modernism is about exposing yourself to other cultures, traveling and learning new things. —*Doug Meyer*

66

Most Glamorous Loft Dining Area
New York City

The late Sergio Savarese and his wife, Monique (cofounders of Dialogica), spent five years working on the 3,500-square-foot SoHo loft they shared with their twin sons before they were satisfied with the results. Typical of the energetic couple's lyrical modernism was this dining room. The mirror, with its hand-carved frame by Sergio, was painted the same color as the walls. "The trees outside are reflected in it," says Monique, "so you are really bringing the outdoors in." The *Afra* table was designed by Sergio. Tragically, the designer was killed, along with his friend Ivan Luini (see No. 80), in a 2006 plane crash.

Best Handmade Bed... And Bedroom... And House
Yakima, Washington

Renowned Native-American artist Leo Adams, a gentle soul whose work finds its inspiration in nature, particularly in wildflowers, inherited his house on the perimeter of the Yakima reservation from his grandfather, a tribal chief, in the early 1970s. Since then, he has added ten rooms and a second story, turning the entire place into a multicultural work of art, creating virtually everything himself from recycled materials. The bed is framed in porch posts and has a canopy "fringe" of recycled cardboard; the bedroom walls are covered in surplus army blankets. Adams actually ages wood outdoors to use in his constantly evolving masterpiece.

68

Best Composition of Naturals and Neutrals
Dallas, Texas

For the house that he built for his client (on the site of her childhood home), architect Max Levy limited himself to just a few simple materials—concrete, stone, wood (mostly fir), and metal. He applied them with such a masterly sense of proportion that the open-plan residence feels serenely perfect, a sense enhanced by the shoji screens on industrial hardware that separate the living spaces. Interior designer Paul Draper helped with the tranquil scheme: The Christian Liaigre *Opium* sofas in the living room are based on Chinese daybeds. All in all, this home could serve as the textbook definition of design equipoise.

69

Most Harmonic Convergence
of Animal, Vegetable, and Minimal
Southampton, New York

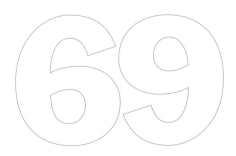

"Natural light is critically important to good architectural design," says William J. Reese, who was hired to create this Long Island getaway for a loft-dwelling Manhattan family with two small boys. It was clear from the beginning that integrating the architecture and the environment was as important to the clients as it was to Reese, so—inspired by the homeowners' fondness for concrete-loving, minimalist Japanese architect Tadao Ando and his own affection for the indoor/outdoor California homes of Rudolph Schindler—Reese pulled the walls out into the cherry orchard, creating a Zen-like equilibrium between the 21st-century home and its considerably older landscape.

70

Best Wide-Open Cookhouse
East Texas

The serenely natural lake house that architect Max Levy created for Dallas clients is a compound of seven pavilions arranged to minimize the home's impact on the wooded site. The main building's kitchen features a custom-made island and pivoting doors used for windows (to preserve energy). The room ends in a screened porch that's a visual continuation of the interior since it's separated from the kitchen by a glass wall up to the gable that seems to disappear into the view. The *Forum* pendant lights are from Eureka Lighting; the chairs are by Dakota Jackson (the interior designer was Nancy Leib).

71

Hippest Take on Builder Standard
Chicago, Illinois

Anne Coyle's clients, a young Google executive and his family, bought a brand-new house, but they wanted something to knock their visitors' socks off. Thinking outside the white box, Coyle added a salvaged grille and faced the fireplace wall with black slate. Then she hung golden de Gournay hand-painted silk wallpaper in the open living/dining room and brought in some timeless pieces of her own to complement the clients' collected midcentury furniture. She went bold with pattern: Greek-key carpeting in the family room, giant paisley wallpaper in the basement, and bamboo-inspired bedroom drapes. ...⋮>

Happily, pattern and decoration and a little **razzle-dazzle** have crept into the modern vocabulary. People love ornament and decoration.—*Jonathan Adler*

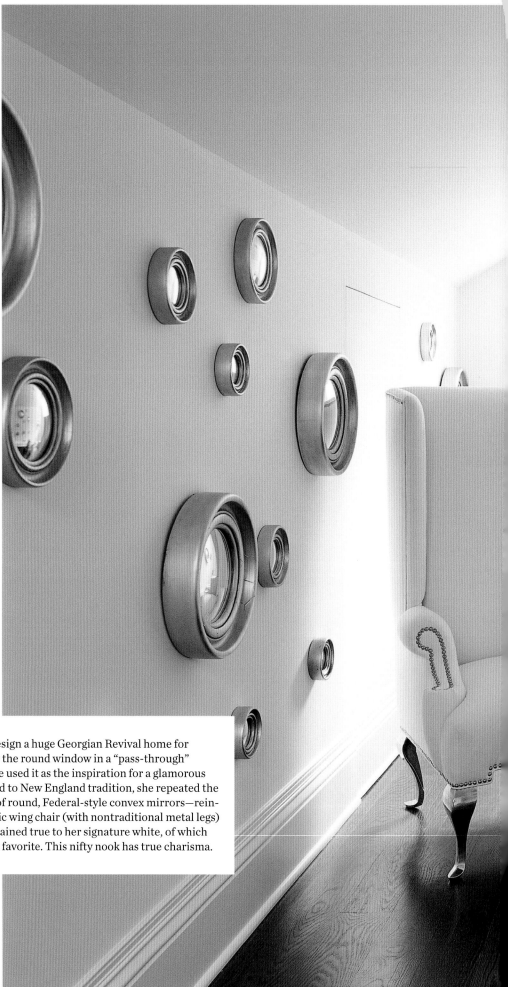

72

Most Enchanting
Secret Passage
Greenwich, Connecticut

When Lynne Scalo was hired to design a huge Georgian Revival home for an active family, she was struck by the round window in a "pass-through" between upstairs bedrooms, so she used it as the inspiration for a glamorous yet comfortable hideaway. As a nod to New England tradition, she repeated the illuminating circle with a collage of round, Federal-style convex mirrors—reinterpreted in silver—adding a classic wing chair (with nontraditional metal legs) and porcelain side tables. She remained true to her signature white, of which Benjamin Moore's *White Dove* is a favorite. This nifty nook has true charisma.

73

Best-Curated Collection
Wilmette, Illinois

When furnishings retailer Fern Simon decided to downsize from a 1920s Mediterranean-style home to a 1970s Wilmette condominium overlooking Lake Michigan, she called on designer Eric Ceputis to help her edit her trove of treasures and shape them into a single living environment. Modernism runs in Simon's family: her twin is Murray Moss, the owner of the trendsetting Moss gallery in Manhattan. Simon's living room features seating by Florence Knoll, a 1940s Paul Frankl cocktail table, and an 1968 Harry Bertoia sculpture; the painting is by Robert Goodnough. Clearly Fern Simon is a major mixologist.

Most Tailored Bedroom
Dallas, Texas

With the help of architect Kenneth Burgess, designers and longtime partners Arthur Johnson and Scott Hill expanded and opened up a two-story postwar house in Dallas, creating a masterful master suite in the process. The bedroom, like the rest of the house, is filled with a pleasingly tranquil mix of masculine pieces in an understated palette. Furnishings mirror the strong linearity of the architecture, with a few softening pieces—like a pair of Ralph Lauren chairs in front of the new fireplace. And perhaps the best feature of the room? Wall-to-wall storage hiding in the built-ins behind a grid of doors, a system that carries into the adjacent master bath.

75

**Best Modernization of a
17th-Century French Manor
Cahors, France**

If you were an English glass designer and a Dutch furniture designer who met in New York, where would you go with the kids to get away from it all? Why, the Lot Valley in southwest France, of course—at least that's where Kate Hume and Frans van der Heyden set up housekeeping, bringing their 21st-century aesthetic to the 15-room house, sympathetically opening it up to light and air. Naturally, they filled it with pieces from their own firm, Birdman Furniture (with the exception of a George Smith *Tiplady Knole* sofa and a woven lounge chair by Marcel Wanders); they accessorized with Hume's striking glass pieces.   ⋯⟩

Modernism is about having a respect for the past but living in the present, with eyes open to what's coming next.—*Fern Simon*

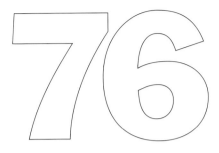

76

Best Bespoke
Bedroom Built-ins
New York City

Color-loving designer Jamie Drake, master of the unrestrained palette, describes this apartment in the Flatiron District of Manhattan as "a venture into the new American glamour—an emotional modernity that is crisp and fresh, yet rich in luster and sexy shapes." And nowhere is this more apparent than in the master bedroom, a monochromatic retreat in muted shades of lilac, lavender, and violet. The headboard wall is upholstered in mohair plush, but the real luxury is the custom storage Drake designed. Monochromatic rooms, says the deluxe designer, are good for people who are a bit timid about color.

Most Amazingly Graceful Screened Porch
Truro, Massachusetts

The house that Boston-based architect Kelly Monnahan and landscape architect Keith LeBlanc built for themselves on Cape Cod is adamantly modern but echoes the shingle vernacular of the peninsula. The house has six decks, plus this dramatic outdoor dining room that stretches out under a soaring gable with deep eaves, its horizontal cedar batons almost Asian in their harmony, although the house owes much of its structure to the tobacco barns Monnahan saw as a child while driving cross-country. The dining furniture, from the 1966 Collection by Richard Schultz, was originally designed for the Florida home of the legendary Florence Knoll.

78

Best Home Built to Accommodate a Canvas
Vancouver, British Columbia, Canada

When Martha Sturdy—designer of jewelry, fabric, furniture, and chic resin housewares—fell in love with a giant painting (right) by Attila Richard Lukacs, Sturdy's husband, David Wardle, joked that they'd need a new house. Sturdy, a fan of the overscaled, had no problem with that, so they contacted Peter Cardew, the British-born architect who designed the gallery where they found the painting, and hired him to create a wide-open home on a West Vancouver hillside overlooking the Georgia Straits. The house is not shy about its presence, but for all its handsomely engineered modernism, this art-filled home has nature at its heart.

79

Best Bathroom that Thinks It's a Gallery
Costa Mesa, California

Husband-and-wife design partners Melissa and Marc Palazzo are used to thinking outside the box. When their family grew, they decided to break out of the confines of their 1950s home, calling in architect Henry Buckingham for a light-filled addition/renovation, an experiment in old meets new. True to Melissa's preferences, the master bath is white, with a crystal chandelier hanging from the skylight grid. In this sanctum, Walker Zanger tile meets tone-on-tone Osborne & Little wallpaper, a tufted George Smith chair, and photographs by Han Lei and Billy & Hells. This private spa really reflects the homeowners, and we're not just talking about their faces in the vanity mirrors.

Most Perfectly Minimal Guest Room
Noyack, New York

Ivan Luini, the Italian-born founder of Kartell, the groundbreaking company that pioneered and popularized plastic furnishings, hired Craig Konyk of Brooklyn to design a family home on eastern Long Island. Appropriately, Konyk made ample use of a recyclable polycarbonate building product to encourage the migration of light. In this room, he paired it with nature's favorite eco-botanical, bamboo, both in the flooring and the wall-to-wall "headboard." For intriguing simplicity, walls, floor, and ceiling meet in recessed aluminum channels, proving there's more to minimalism than immediately meets the eye. Sadly, Luini died, along with Sergio Savarese (see No. 66) in a 2006 plane crash.

81

Best Little Cabin in the Woods
Skykomish, Washington

Tom Kundig, of Olson Kundig Architects, is one of the most forward-looking and most honored architects in the country, having won wide recognition for an artful respect for the environment as well as a refreshing modesty. Of the client for this meditative 575-square-foot riverside cabin in the Cascades, Kundig says, "He's not here to be in architecture; he's here to be in nature." The steel-clad cabin features floor-to-ceiling glass doors framed in salvaged fir that open to eradicate the walls, turning the place into what is essentially a sophisticated platform with a roof. This home-away-from-home is a natural treasure. ⋯⋗

Modernism is characterized by an intersection of the rational and the poetic.
—*Tom Kundig*

82

Best Modern Flat in a Second-Empire Building
Paris, France

Designer Christian Duc—born in Asia, raised in the U.S., and educated in Europe—was looking for a home with three luxuries: space, light, and calm. The archetypal modernist was surprised to be taken with an abandoned office (offered for sale without a kitchen or bathroom) in an 1860s building in the 10th Arrondissement. It may have been abused by long commercial use, but it had glorious natural light and a lot of residential potential. Evolving from his former black-and-white, hard-edged modernist mode to a softer conjunction of East and West, Duc now finds "comfort and natural warmth through wood, leather, linen, and silk in shades of beige and brown." We couldn't agree more.

Best Homage to Hermès Orange
Santa Monica, California

In the design world, Michael Smith is as well known as his high-profile clients, folks like, well, the Obamas of Illinois and Washington, D.C. Impressed by his signature balance of the historic and the contemporary, the president and his wife hired Smith to personalize their rooms in the White House. Meanwhile, back in his own apartment (circa 1996), Smith took on the challenge of orange, "every designer's least favorite color" and made it work with furniture of his own design, accented with favorite pieces from the U.S., Europe, and the Far East. If you like an elegant "Big Mix," you don't have to look further than this for inspiration.

84

Best Place to Entertain a Cougar
La Crescenta, California

A year after artists Lari Pittman and Roy Dowell moved in to their tiny Richard Neutra house in the hilly suburbs of L.A., they realized the place they loved was too small for serious entertaining. They called on a friend, architect Roger F. White, to create an outdoor entertaining space on a flat parcel of adjacent land. White designed a floating "ode to minimalism," a deck made of Trex (recycled plastic), topped with a pavilion that houses a fully equipped kitchen. Then Pittman and Dowel created a "French rationalist" garden ... with cacti and California pepper trees. Uninvited guests have included neighboring mountain felines.

Best Way to Float a Mortgage
Seattle, Washington

If you've ever fantasized about a house near the water, consider this modern charmer, which sits on the surface. It's a houseboat designed for a couple who live in Sun Valley, Idaho. Jokes one of the owners, "I've always said I wanted a cabin on a lake in the middle of a city," and that's essentially what this Lake Union floating home turned out to be. The owners wanted the houseboat lifestyle but without any of the usual Victorian gingerbread, so modernist architect Tim Carlander was a perfect choice to maximize space and comfort in a contemporary mode, creating a see-worthy getaway in the process.

86

Best Reuse of an Obsolete Commercial Building
Chicago, Illinois

Years of conversions have taken most of the guesswork out of transforming disused industrial buildings into residential lofts, but those precedents didn't help much when Laurence O. Booth was hired to turn a brick chicken rendering plant in South Lakeview into a live/work space for a Chicago couple. Booth's meticulous detailing in renovating the original building brought refinement to the equation; then he added a family room/kitchen wing bracketed by an entry courtyard in front and a patio out back. An upstairs terrace is reached by a spiral staircase in the old smokestack, and there's an indoor pool, too—upstairs, adjacent to the master bath. Be careful where you sleepwalk. ⋯⋗

Modern can breathe. Modern is open. Modern leans toward simplicity. It's a complex simplicity, but it's easy on the eye. —*John Lyle*

Best Living Room
with a Library in It
Seattle, Washington

For the gut remodel of a 1971 house in Seattle, Tom Kundig, of renowned Olson Kundig Architects, employed one of his favorite materials: "Steel can transform the ordinary into something special," he says. For the combined living room, dining room, music room, and library, he designed a fireplace (fabricated by David Gulassa) that commands the space by understatement. It faces (on the other side of the room) a seven-by-nine-foot pivot door of the same material that leads to the kitchen. The light and dark neutrals create a satisfying serenity, which is the name the owner gave to the custom-mixed paint color.

89

Best Example of Going with the Grain
Minneapolis, Minnesota

Before the renovation, this invitingly modern open home was a New England–style cottage with multiple add-ons. Although charming outside, the confining configuration of rooms served to keep the close family of five apart. Then the modern bug bit. In came Julie Snow Architects, who added a screened porch and bumped out the living room, but otherwise worked in the existing footprint, radically rearranging the floor plan. Furnishings are a textural play on light and dark—much of that light coming through a high-efficiency commercial window system. Now the house is as open to its residents as they are to one another.

Best Copper-Clad Fireplace
Los Angeles, California

Architect William Hefner designed this family house to maximize the light, but the living room, created with designer Kazuko Hoshino (who happens to be Hefner's wife as well as his business partner and constant collaborator), is a darker, meditative space with walnut walls and ceiling and a copper-clad fireplace with a contrasting travertine mantel (the art is by Darren Waterson). Vaguely Asian and definitely modern, the room pairs a Christian Liaigre sofa with vintage chairs and a table made from an antique door. The harmony here comes from the balance of neutrals and the warmth of the natural materials.

Best Example of Keeping It Simple
Chicago, Illinois

Architect Patrizio Fradiani had a problem: A dowdy Victorian in Chicago's Ravenswood neighborhood and a sleek, modern Italian design sensibility. He loves the Milanese aesthetic, but the house had its own integrity, which meant blending the two seemingly irreconcilable differences. So he respected the house, but furnished it his way. He brightened the perfectly symmetrical dining room with new glass-paneled doors, removed the heavy plaster ceiling, and refinished the original pine floors, proving that less is certainly more. The jolt of the new is in the furnishings: a hanging Flos fixture, a Fantoni desk used as a table, and *Catifa* chairs from Arper.

92

Most On-Point Makeover
of an Eichler Original
San Rafael, California

When a retired ballet dancer (now in real estate) realized her dream by buying a home built by midcentury legend Joseph Eichler, she hired Marek Slosar and Lucian Rosciszewski to update the place while respecting its perfect pas de deux of indoors and out. The post-and-beam house, which is built as a series of rooms around an open courtyard, was stripped down to pure geometry and furnished with a minimalist romp through variations on white that introduces Bauhaus linearity to the curves of a dancer's body. Most of the living room furniture is by Jean-Marie Massaud. The flow of light is positively terpsichorean. ⋯⟩

215

I always tell my students to think of **light as a material.**—*Carlos Martinez*

93

Best Living Room Inspired by the Ark
Lakes District, New Hampshire

The house that Michael Kim built for his clients, a Massachusetts family of five, combines their love of glass houses à la Mies van der Rohe and traditional lap-strake-constructed boats that were once common on the adjacent lake (the site used to be a summer camp). The house includes this soaring great room with a 12-foot-high split-granite fireplace and a ceiling that looks like a hull. Boston-based designer Frank Roop created the custom furniture, which is covered in fade-resistant, kid-friendly fabrics (like linens and leathers); the chairs—big enough for an adult and one child—are perfect refuges from any storm.

Best Primary Palette
Brooklyn, New York

Interior designer Christopher Coleman (a former display director of Macy's) loves color; his partner, fashion designer Angel Sanchez, who is a trained architect, is not quite as committed to the Crayola box. Decorating their own environment—a newly minted, 1,175-square-foot loft in the bohemian-hip Williamsburg neighborhood, involved some chromatic negotiation. The two, who have collaborated on numerous design projects, struck a balance with a limited number of colors set against liberal expanses of white. The wallpaper Coleman designed for the kitchen was inspired by the work of 1950s Venezuelan artist Alejandro Otero. The table is also Coleman's; the chairs are by Gio Ponti.

95

Best Master Bath in Britain
Kintbury, Berkshire, U.K.

In the U.K., Sir Terence Conran is king of the modern home furnishings hill—
not to mention an A-list restaurateur, hotelier, writer, publisher, and the father
of a brood of successful designers. So when he renovated Barton Court, the
18th-century home he shares with his wife, Vicki, the master bath had to be fit
for royalty. Previously, says Sir T, it was "old-fashioned and uncomfortable."
Now it's altogether new, not to mention sybaritic, and at 30 by 30 feet, it's
almost as big as Bath, the city. It gives new meaning to luxuriating in a long, hot
soak (the tub is Victorian, the sofa a Conran design, the lamp by Ingo Maurer).

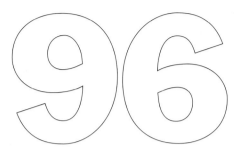

96

Best Way to Suspend Disbelief
Washington, D.C.

Travis Price is not just a modernist architect. He's a philosopher and something of a poet, to boot. For his own home on a leafy block of revivalist houses
that backs onto Rock Creek Park, Price opted for an almost Russian Construc-
tivist building. To reduce its impact on the earth, the house was engineered to
be hung from a massive central "tent pole," instead of sitting on an intrusive
concrete foundation (Price even built a jog into the front wall to preserve an
old tree). The ecologically green house has a street façade clad in a patinated
copper that makes the whole house recede visually into the verdant foliage.

97

Best Hillside Home
in the Rockies
Aspen, Colorado

Architect Hugh Newell Jacobsen, who works out of Washington, D.C., has spent a 300-house career making residences from arrangements of components he calls "Monopoly houses." Pure in vernacular form, yet pared down sufficiently to read instantly as modern, the pavilions are united visually by architectural details. The pearls in this alpine string are arranged around a 100-foot-long glassed-in hallway. At 30 feet high, the living room is the tallest, but all the rooms are composed around the views of the outside and of other interior spaces. The pitched roofs echo the Rockies just beyond the windows. ⋯⋗

The most elementary act of modern architecture is the **framing of a view**, even in a seemingly hopeless setting. That view can be a single flower or a sliver of sky.—*Max Levy*

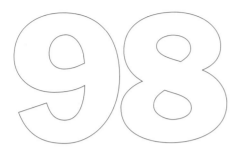

98

Best Home Above the Store
San Francisco, California

Dan Friedlander is known in the design industry for LIMN, his pioneering
South of Market museumlike furniture store. An early champion of design
stars like Philippe Starck and the Memphis group around Ettore Sottsass,
Friedlander designed his own home on the same property, creating a stunning
modern space with a soaring living room wall that contains 36 square windows
in a perfect grid. He filled his home with the kind of furniture treasures on sale
downstairs. The living room alone (circa 1997) contains pieces by Maxalto,
B&B Italia, Ligne Roset, Herman Miller, Cassina, Moltana, and Zanotta.

When you walk, just walk; when you eat, just eat.

99

Most Out-of-the-Box Kitchen
New Orleans, Louisiana

The century-old home that designer Jill Dupré shares with her family in the Bayou St. John neighborhood of the Big Easy has a hallway that runs from the front door to the back, with rooms lined up on either side. That was fine as far as it went, but to open, lighten, and modernize the house, Dupré took down the walls at the back of the house, leaving a completely open kitchen to face an open den across a double row of fluted pillars where the walls used to be. The 12-foot-long all-purpose island has drawers within drawers for storage; the backsplash contrasts white ceramic subway tiles with stainless-steel minis.

Most Masterly Millwork in Manhattan
New York City

The Park Avenue apartment conceived by Maya Lin for a record executive and his family is an exercise in ingenuity. Working with architect David Hotson and designer Alan Tanksley, Lin restructured the 40-foot-by-100-foot gutted space with a magician's skill. The embracing and quietly dramatic millwork (all of it clad in American brown oak veneer) is more than decorative: It hides doors and drawers, cabinets and storage cubbies; it even holds an aquarium. One whole wall of shelves, television included, pivots open between the bedroom and the den. Lin endowed this place with the same refinement she brought to the Vietnam War Memorial.

Contacts and Credits

1
Design: Elaine Cecconi
Cecconi Simone
1335 Dundas Street West
Toronto, Ontario M6J 1Y3 Canada
416/588-5900
www.cecconisimone.com
Produced by Linda O'Keeffe
Original story written by Lucie Young
Photography by Ted Yarwood

2
Design: Jonathan Adler
333 Hudson Street, Suite 1004
New York, NY 10013
212/645-2802
www.jonathanadler.com
Produced by Linda O'Keeffe
Photography by Joshua McHugh

3
Design: Feroza Jonuschat
and Katja Wilkens
Bulthaup New York
158 Wooster Street
New York, NY 10012
212/966-7183
www.bulthaup.com
Produced by Elana Frankel
Original story written by Susan Kleinman
Photography by Jeff McNamara

4
Architecture: Gokhan Avcioglu
Global Architectural Development/GAD
29 Broadway, Suite 1506
New York, NY 10006
917/338-1395
www.gadarchitecture.com
Design: Lori Graham
Lori Graham Design
1604 17th Street NW
Washington, DC 20009
202/745-0118
www.lorigrahamdesign.com
Produced by Susan Tyree Victoria
and Barbara Bohl
Original story written by Gregory Cerio
Photography by Erik Johnson

5
Design: Valerie Pasquiou
and Constance Delorme
Valerie Pasquiou Interiors + Design, Inc.
47 Ann Street
New York, NY 10038
212/227-3983
and
VPID/C L'Agence (Gaspard Ronjat)
159 rue Montmartre
75002 Paris, France
+33(0)1.77.72.77.72
www.vpinteriors.com
Produced by Linda O'Keeffe
Original story written by Susan Morgan
Photography by Grey Crawford

6
Design: Darryl Wilson
Darryl Wilson Design/Development
8440 Santa Monica Boulevard,
Suite 101
West Hollywood, CA 90069
www.darrylwilsondesign.com
Produced by Elana Frankel and Laura Hull
Original story written by Michael Lassell
Photography by Jonn Coolidge

7
Architecture/Design: E. B. Min
and Jeffrey Day
Min | Day
2325 Third Street, No. 425
San Francisco, CA 94107
415/255-9464
and
5912 Maple Street
Omaha, NE 68104
402/551-0306
www.minday.com
Produced by Susan Tyree Victoria
Original story written by Fred A. Bernstein
Photography by John Reed Forsman

8
Architecture: William E. Bennett
24 Brant Road North
Cambridge, Ontario N1S 2W1 Canada
519/624-3200
bbennett@langdonhall.com
Design: Powell & Bonnell Design
Consultants
236 Davenport Road
Toronto, Ontario M5R 1J6 Canada
416/964-6210
www.powellandbonnell.com
Produced by Linda O'Keeffe
Original story written by Fred A. Bernstein
Photography by Ted Yarwood

9
Design: Karim Rashid
357 W. 17th Street
New York, NY 10011
212/929-8657
www.karimrashid.com
Produced by Linda O'Keeffe
Original story written by Lucie Young
Photography by Antoine Bootz

10
Architecture: Tim Andreas
Banjo Architecture & Design
1311 Angelus Avenue
Los Angeles, CA 90026
323/666-3826
www.banjoad.com
Produced by Donna Warner
Original story written by Fred A. Bernstein
Photography by Dominique Vorillon

11
Design: Carlos Martinez
Gensler
11 E. Madison Street
Chicago, IL 60602
312/456-0123
www.gensler.com
Produced by Linda O'Keeffe
and Lisa Skolnik
Original story written by Michael Lassell
Photography by Antoine Bootz

12
Design: Doug Meyer
Doug & Gene Meyer Studio
30 NE 40th Street
Miami, FL 33137
305/458-2439
www.dougandgenemeyer.com
Produced by Linda O'Keeffe
Original story written by Beth Dunlop
Photography by Mark Roskams

13
Design: Richard Ferretti
and James Gager
Contractor: Brett King
Brett King Builder-Contractor, Inc.
7843 Richlandtown Road
Quakertown, PA 18951
215/536-1145
www.brettkingbuilder.com
Produced by Elana Frankel
Original story written by Elaine Greene
Photography by Catherine Tighe

14
Architecture: Douglas Burnham,
Claire Bigbie, Patrick Flynn,
Grayson Holden, Jonathan King
envelope Architecture + Design
1661 20th Street, No. 1
Oakland, CA 94607
510/839-0140
www.envelopead.com
Produced by Jody Kennedy
Photography by Matthew Millman

15
Design: Todd Oldham
Todd Oldham Studio
20 Vesey Street, Suite 200
New York, NY 10007
212/226-4688
www.toddoldham.com
Produced by Linda O'Keeffe
Original story written by Fred A. Bernstein
Photography by Todd Oldham

16
Design: Vivienne Tam
Produced by Linda O'Keeffe
Original story written by Wendy Israel
Photography by John Hall

17
Architecture:
Callas Shortridge Architects
Steven Shortridge
Shortridge Architects
1727 Berkeley Street, Studio 6
Santa Monica, CA 90404
310/829-1460
www.shortridgearchitects.com
Design: Carole Katleman
Carole Katleman Interiors
1320 Carla Lane
Beverly Hills, CA 90210
310/248-2464
Produced by Linda O'Keeffe
and Laura Hull
Original story written by Susan Morgan
Photography by Grey Crawford

18
Design: William Diamond
and Anthony Baratta
Diamond Baratta Design
270 Lafayette Street
New York, NY 10012
212/966-8892
www.diamondbarattadesign.com
Produced by Linda O'Keeffe
Original story written by Fred A. Bernstein
Photography by Jeff McNamara

19
Architecture: Philip Johnson
Produced by Donna Warner
Original story written by Joseph Giovannini
Photography by Michael Luppino

20
Design: Ronald Bricke
Ronald Bricke & Associates
333 E. 69th Street
New York, NY 10021
212/472-9006
www.ronaldbricke.com
Produced by Linda O'Keeffe
Original story written by Fred Albert
Photography by Grey Crawford

21
Produced by Linda O'Keeffe
and Lisa Skolnik
Original story written by Lisa Skolnik
Photography by Nathan Kirkman

22
Architecture/Design: Larry Totah
Totah Design
1022 Palm Avenue, Suite 3
West Hollywood, CA 90069
310/289-0700
www.totahdesign.com
Produced by Newell Turner
Original story written by Leah Rosch
Photography by Grey Crawford

23
Architecture: Ettore Sottsass
with Johanna Grawunder
Sottsass Associati
Via Melone 2
20121 Milan, Italy
+39/0289866100
www.sottsass.it
Produced by Donna Warner
Original story written by Michael Lassell
Photography by Grey Crawford

24
Architecture: Peter Madimenos
Adimé Architecture
6430 N. Olympia Avenue
Chicago, IL 60631
773/594-1610
www.adime.com
Design: Kara Mann and Kristin Nelson
Kara Mann Design
119 W. Hubbard Street, 5th floor
Chicago, IL 60654
312/893-7550
www.karamann.com
Produced by Susan Tyree Victoria
and Lisa Skolnik
Original story written by Lisa Skolnik
Photography by Nathan Kirkman

25
Architecture: Jim Poteet, Brett Freeman
Poteet Architects
1114 S. St. Marys Street, Suite 100
San Antonio, TX 78210
210/281-9818
www.poteetarchitects.com
and
Patrick Ousey
FAB Architecture
402 Josephine Street
Austin, TX 78704
512/469-0775
www.fabarchitecture.com
Produced by Susan Tyree Victoria and
Helen Thompson
Original story written by Helen Thompson
Photography by Colleen Duffley

26
Design: Peter Hawrylewicz
Architecture: Hawrylewicz & Robertson
Architecture and Design
1680 Michigan Avenue
Miami Beach, FL 33139
305/672-5658
Produced by Newell Turner
Original story written by Richard Martin
Photography by Tim Street-Porter

27
Architecture: Carl Magnusson
Magnusson Design & Building
625 Edgecliff Drive
Langley, WA 98260
360/221-6932
cdmdbsampling.wordpress.com
Produced by Linda O'Keeffe
and Linda Humphrey
Original story written by Valerie Easton
Photography by John Granen

28
Design: Glenn Heim
Produced by Linda O'Keeffe
and Nisi Berryman
Original story written by Beth Dunlop
Photography by Quentin Bacon

29
Design: Kelly Wearstler
Kelly Wearstler Studio
760 N. La Cienega Boulevard
Los Angeles, CA 90069
323/951-7454
www.kellywearstler.com
Original story written by Susan Morgan
Photography courtesy of Kelly Wearstler
Studio

30
Architecture/Design:
Jean-Michel Wilmotte
Wilmotte & Associés
68 rue Faubourg Saint-Antoine
75012 Paris, France
+33(0)1.53.02.22.22
www.wilmotte.fr
Produced by Jean Bond Rafferty
Original story written by Jean
Bond Rafferty
Photography by Didi von Schaewen

31
Design: John Lyle
John Lyle Design
P.O. Box 1567
New York, NY 10150
646/344-1964
www.johnlyledesign.com
Produced by Susan Tyree Victoria
Original story written by Fred Albert
Photography by Jack Thompson

32
Architecture: Clint Pehrson Architects
216 Highland Drive
Seattle, WA 98109
206/621-1298
Produced by Doretta Sperduto
and Linda Humphrey
Original story written by Jeff Book
Photography by Martin Tessler

33
Design: Toby Zack
Toby Zack Designs
3316 Griffin Road
Fort Lauderdale, FL 33312
954/967-8629
www.tobyzackdesigns.com
Produced by Linda O'Keeffe
and Nisi Berryman
Original story written by Jeff Book
Photography by Carlos Domenech

34
Architecture: Ron Mason
Anderson Mason Dale Architects
3198 Speer Boulevard
Denver, CO 80211
303/294-9448
www.amdarchitects.com
Original story written by Mindy Pantiel
Photography by Frank Ooms

35
Design: Barbara Barry
Barbara Barry Inc.
9526 Pico Boulevard
Los Angeles, CA 90035
310/276-9977
www.barbarabarry.com
Produced by Linda O'Keeffe
Original story written by Susan Morgan
Photography by Jeremy Samuelson

36
Architecture: Marmol Radziner
12210 Nebraska Avenue
Los Angeles, CA 90025
310/826-6222
www.marmol-radziner.com
Produced by Laura Hull
Original story written by Fred A. Bernstein
Photography by Jeremy Samuelson

37
Design: Ann Holden
Holden & Dupuy
839 Saint Charles Avenue, Suite 310
New Orleans, LA 70130
504/568-1101
Produced by Linda O'Keeffe
and Ellen Johnson
Original story written by Kathleen Beckett
Photography by Jeff McNamara

38
Architecture/Design:
Christopher Raphael and
Peggy Wanamaker
Wanamaker Raphael Architecture
1208 Coastal Road
Brooksville, ME 04617
207/326-8235
www.wanamakerraphael.com
Produced by Doretta Sperduto
Original story written by Fred A. Bernstein
Photography by Jeff McNamara

39
Design: Benjamin Noriega-Ortiz
BNO Design
75 Spring Street, 6th floor
New York, NY 10012
212/343-9709
www.bnodesign.com
Produced by Linda O'Keeffe
Original story written by Cara Greenberg
Photography by Antoine Bootz

40
Landscape Design: Linda Iverson
Linda Iverson Landscape Design
1270 Lower Sweet Grass Road
Big Timber, MT 59011
406/932-5840
Landscape Contractor:
Native Landscapes and Reclamation
Box 843
5132 Highway 89 South
Livingston, MT 59047
406/222-0457
Produced by Susan Tyree Victoria
Original story written by Sarah Belk King
Photography by Tom Ferris

41
Architecture: Charles Bohl III
Design: Barbara Bohl
Bohl Architects
161 Prince George Street
Annapolis, MD 21401
410/263-2200
and
8750 Hillside Avenue
Los Angeles, CA 90069
323/848-8800
www.bohlarchitects.com
Produced by Linda O'Keeffe
Original story written by Fred A. Bernstein
Photography by Catherine Tighe

42
Architecture: David Nicolay
Evoke International Design
2388 Alberta Street
Vancouver, BC V5Y 3K7 Canada
604/875-8667
www.evoke.ca
Produced by Linda O'Keeffe
Original story written by Megan O'Neill
Photography by Martin Kessler

43
Architecture: Robert Siegel
Robert Siegel Architects
37 W. 37th Street
New York, NY 10018
212/921-5600
www.robertsiegelarchitects.com
Produced by Elana Frankel
Original story written by Raul Barreneche
Photography by Formula Z/S

44
Design: Vicente Wolf
Vicente Wolf Associates
333 W. 39th Street
New York, NY 10018
212/465-0590
www.vicentewolf.com
Produced by Linda O'Keeffe
Original story written by Fred A. Bernstein
Photography by Vicente Wolf

45
Design: Marjorie Skouras
2915 N. Beachwood Drive
Hollywood, CA 90068
323/469-3636
www.marjorieskourasdesign.com
Produced by Linda O'Keeffe
and Laura Hull
Original story written by Susan Morgan
Photography by John Ellis

46
Design: Cheryl and Jeffrey Katz
C&J Katz Studio
60 K Street
South Boston, MA 02127
617/464-0330
www.candjkatz.com
Produced by Newell Turner
and Donna Paul
Original story written by Liz Seymour
Photography by Pieter Estersohn

47
Architecture/Design: Alison Spear AIA
P.O. Box 360
Hughsonville, NY 12537
845/298-0888
www.alisonspearaia.com
Produced by Linda O'Keeffe
and Laura Hull
Original story written by Hunter
Drohojowska-Philp
Photography by Jonn Coolidge

48
Architects: Marsha Maytum
Leddy Maytum Stacy Architects
677 Harrison Street
San Francisco, CA 94107
415/495-1700
www.lmsarch.com
Produced by Linda O'Keeffe
Original story written by Aaron Betsky
Photography by Luis Gordoa

49
Design: Kelly Hoppen
Kelly Hoppen Interiors
102A Chepstow Road
St. Stephen's Yard
London W2 5QW U.K.
+44(0)207-471-3350
3350
www.kellyhoppen.com
Produced by Linda O'Keeffe
Original story written by Linda O'Keeffe
Photography by David Garcia

50
Architecture/Design:
Philip Michael Wolfson
Wolfson Design
Belletowers, 7E
16 Island Avenue
Miami Beach, FL 33139
305/532-4793
and
24 Palace Court, Studio 11A
London W2 4HU U.K.
+44(0)207-229-3221
www.wolfsondesign.com
Produced by Linda O'Keeffe
and Nisi Berryman
Original story written by Beth Dunlop
Photography by Carlos Domenech

51
Design: Eric Ceputis
Eric Ceputis Design
701 Ingleside Place
Evanston, IL 60201
847/864-1124
and **Harriet Robinson**
Harriet Robinson Interior Design
900 Pine Tree Lane
Winnetka, IL 60093
847/446-2590
Produced by Susan Tyree Victoria
and Lisa Skolnik
Original story written by Lisa Skolnik
Photography by Nathan Kirkman

52
Design: Darryl Carter
202/234-5926
www.darrylcarter.com
Produced by Susan Tyree Victoria
and Barbara Bohl
Original story written by Mario
López-Cordero
Photography by Gordon Beall

53
Design: Gregory Dufner and Daniel
Heighes Wismer
Dufner Heighes
195 Chrystie Street, No. 801D
New York, NY 10002
212/420-1605
www.dufnerheighes.com
Produced by Elana Frankel
Original story written by Elaine Greene
Photography by John Ellis

54
Design: Christopher Ciccone
www.christophergciccone.com
Produced by Linda O'Keeffe
Original story written by Linda O'Keeffe
Photography by Michael Luppino

55
Original architecture: Frank Lloyd Wright
Renovation Architecture:
John Rattenbury
Design: Mil Bodron
Bodron + Fruit
4040 N. Central Expressway, Suite 150
Dallas, TX 75204
214/826-5200
www.bodronfruit.com
Produced by Donna Warner
Original story written by Fred A. Bernstein
Photography by Tim Street-Porter

56
Produced by Linda O'Keeffe
Original story written by Fred A. Bernstein
Photography by Tim Street-Porter

57
Design: Betsey Johnson
Produced by Linda O'Keeffe
Original story written by
Michael Cunningham
Photography by Maura McEvoy

58
Architecture: Brian Messana
and Toby O'Rorke
Messana O'Rorke Architects
118 W. 22nd Street, 9th Floor
New York, NY 10011
212/807-1960
www.brianmessana.com
Produced by Linda O'Keeffe
Original story written by Fred A. Bernstein
Photography by Michael Grimm

59
Architecture: Scott Joyce
Scott Joyce Design
6415 W. Rodgerton Drive
Hollywood, CA 90068
323/463-4644
www.scottjoycedesign.com
Exterior Design: Tory Polone
310/721-2861
www.torypolone.com
Interior Design: Susan Young
Susan Young Interiors
5833 6th Avenue S.
Seattle, WA 98108
206/467-6869
www.susanyounginteriors.com
Produced by Laura Hull
Original story written by Fred A. Bernstein
Photography by John Ellis

60
Design: William Sawaya
Sawaya & Moroni
Via Andegari, 18 / via Manzoni 11
20121 Milan, Italy
+39-02-86-395-212
www.sawayamoroni.com
Original story written by Arlene Hirst
Photography by Armando Bertacchi

61
Architecture: Rick Archer, principal;
Todd Walbourn, project architect
Overland Partners Architects
5101 Broadway
San Antonio, TX 78209
210/829-7003
www.overlandpartners.com
Design: Emily Summers
Emily Summers Design Associates
4639 Insurance Lane
Dallas, TX 75205
214/871-9669
www.emilysummers.com
Produced by Doretta Sperduto
and Helen Thompson
Original story written by Helen Thompson
Photography by Jeff McNamara

62
Design: Larry Laslo
Larry Laslo Designs
240 E. 67th Street, Suite A
New York, NY 10065
212/734-3824
www.larrylaslodesigns.com
Produced by Linda O'Keeffe
and Nisi Berryman
Original story written by Beth Dunlop
Photography by Ken Hayden

63
Design: D. Crosby Ross
9200 West Sunset Boulevard
West Hollywood, CA 90069
310/859-7320
Produced by Linda O'Keeffe
Original story written by Susan Morgan
Photography by David Glomb

64
**Architecture: David Lake, Ted Flato
and Graham Martin
Lake|Flato Architects**
311 Third Street
San Antonio, TX 78205
210/227-3335
www.lakeflato.com
*Produced by Timothy J. Ward
with Susan Weinberger
Original story written by Julie V. Iovine
Photography by Langdon Clay*

65
Design: Dale Chihuly
*Produced by Linda O'Keeffe
and Linda Humphrey
Original story written by Fred Albert
Photography by John Granen*

66
Design: Monique and Sergio Savarese
*Produced by Elana Frankel
Original story written by Arlene Hirst
Photography by Peter Murdock*

67
Design by Leo Adams
*Produced by Linda O'Keeffe
and Linda Humphrey
Original story written by Fred A. Bernstein
Photography by Jonn Coolidge*

68
Architecture: Max Levy, FAIA
5646 Milton Street
Dallas, TX 75206
214/368-2023
www.maxlevyarchitect.com
**Design: Paul Draper
Draper + Associates**
4106 Swiss Avenue
Dallas, TX 75204
214/824-8352
*Produced by Elana Frankel
and Diane Carroll
Original story written by Fred A. Bernstein
Photography by Colleen Duffley*

69
Architecture: William J. Reese
41 Meetinghouse Lane
Southampton, NY 11968
631/899-4320
and
7811 Eads Avenue, # 311
La Jolla, CA 92037
858/246-7710
www.wjreese.net
*Produced by Susan Tyree Victoria
Original story written by Fred A. Bernstein
Photography by Antoine Bootz*

70
Architecture: Max Levy
5646 Milton Street, Suite 709
Dallas, TX 75206
214/368-2023
www.maxlevyarchitect.com
Design: Nancy G. Leib
5646 Milton Street, Suite 888
Dallas, TX 75206
214/696-2231
www.pd-nl.com
*Produced by Diane Carroll
Original story written by Diane Carroll
Photography by Jack Thompson*

71
**Design: Anne Coyle
Anne Coyle Interiors**
2041 W. Wabansia Avenue
Chicago, IL 60647
773/235-6131
www.annecoyleinteriors.com
*Produced by Susan Tyree Victoria
and Lisa Skolnik
Photography by Nathan Kirkman*

72
Design: Lynne Scalo
23 Jesup Road
Westport, CT 06880
203/222-4991
www.lynnescalo.com
*Produced by Susan Tyree Victoria
Photography by Tim Street-Porter*

73
**Design: Fern Simon and Eric Ceputis
Arts 220**
895½ Green Bay Road
Winnetka, IL 60093
847/501.3084
www.arts220.com
*Produced by Susan Tyree Victoria
and Lisa Skolnik
Original story written by Lisa Skolnik
Photography by Nathan Kirkman*

74
**Design: Arthur Johnson and Scott Hill
Square One Furniture**
6919 N. Janmar Drive
Dallas, TX 75230
214/599-0266
www.squareonefurniture.blogspot.com
*Produced by Newell Turner
and Diane Carroll
Original story written by Helen Thompson
Photography by Grey Crawford*

75
**Design: Kate Hume
and Frans van der Heyden**
Eerste Weteringdwarsstraat 81
1017 Amsterdam TM, Netherlands
+31-20-625-3522
www.katehume.com
*Produced by Linda O'Keeffe
and Jean Bond Rafferty
Original story written
by Jean Bond Rafferty
Photography by Frans van der Heyden*

76
**Design: Jamie Drake
Drake Design Associates**
315 E. 62nd Street
New York, NY 10021
212/754-3099
www.drakedesignassociates.com
*Produced by Linda O'Keeffe
Original story written by Elaine Greene
Photography by Bruce Buck*

77
**Architecture/Design: Kelly Monnahan
Kelly Monnahan Design**
535 Albany Street, Suite 5A
Boston, MA 02118
617/778-6475
www.kellymonnahan.com
**Landscape: Keith LeBlanc
Keith LeBlanc Landscape
Architecture Inc.**
535 Albany Street, Suite 5A
Boston, MA 02118
617/426.6475
www.kl-la.com
*Produced by Doretta Sperduto
Original story written by Lucie Young
Photography by Sang An*

78
**Architecture: Peter Cardew
Peter Cardew Architects**
430 Railway Street
Vancouver, BC V6A 1B1, Canada
604/681-6044
www.cardew.ca
*Produced by Linda O'Keeffe
Original story written by Aaron Betsky
Photography by Martin Kessler*

79
**Architecture: Henry Beckingham
METER**
460 S. Spring Street, No. 1211
Los Angeles, CA 90013
323/791-1468
**Design: Melissa Palazzo
Pal + Smith**
20321 Irvine Avenue, Building E
Newport Beach, CA 92707
888/725-7684
www.palandsmith.com
*Produced by Linda O'Keeffe
and Laura Hull
Original story written by Fred A. Bernstein
Photography by John Ellis*

80
**Architecture: Craig Konyk,
Armando Petruccelli, Hyunkil Son
Konyk Architecture**
P.O. Box 22546
Brooklyn, NY 11202
718/852-5381
www.konyk.net
*Produced by Donna Warner
Original story written by Fred A. Bernstein
Photography by Michael Luppino*

81
**Architecture: Tom Kundig
Olson Kundig Architects**
159 S. Jackson Street, Suite 600
Seattle, WA 98104
206/624-5670
www.olsonkundigarchitects.com
*Produced by Linda O'Keeffe
and Linda Humphrey
Original story written by Fred Albert
Photography by John Granen*

82
Design: Christian Duc
68 rue d'Hauteville
75010 Paris, France
+33(0)1.47.70.03.45
www.christianduc.fr
*Produced by Jean Bond Rafferty
Original story written by Jean
Bond Rafferty
Photography by Didi von Schaewen*

83
Design: Michael S. Smith
1646 19th Street
Santa Monica, CA 90404
310/315-3018
www.michaelsmithinc.com
Produced by Diane Dorrans Saeks
Original story written by Jeff Book
Photography by Michael Mundy

84
Architecture: Roger Faulds White
Roger F. White Studio
343 5th Avenue
Venice, CA 90291
310/399-4187
Produced by Elana Frankel and Laura Hull
Original story written by Hunter
Drohojowska-Philp
Photography by Tim Street-Porter

85
Architecture: Tim Carlander
Vanderventer + Carlander Architects
2727 Western Avenue
Seattle, WA 98121
206/323-8770
www.vc-arch.com
Produced by Linda O'Keeffe
and Linda Humphrey
Original story written by Fred Albert
Photography by John Granen

86
Architecture: Laurence O. Booth
Booth Hansen
333 S. DesPlaines Street
Chicago, IL 60661
312/869-5000
www.boothhansen.com
Produced by Linda O'Keeffe
and Lisa Skolnik
Original story written by Michael Lassell
Photography by Antoine Bootz

87
Architecture: Tom Kundig
Olson Kundig Architects
159 S. Jackson Street, Suite 600
Seattle, WA 98104
206/624-5670
www.olsonkundigarchitects.com
Produced by Linda O'Keeffe
and Linda Humphrey
Original story written by Mathew Stadler
Photography by Grey Crawford

88
Design: Frank Roop
Frank Roop Design Interiors
224 Clarendon Street, Suite 31
Boston, MA 02116
617/267-0818
www.frankroop.com
Produced by Susan Tyree Victoria
Original story written by Rachel Levitt
Photography by Eric Roth

89
Architecture/Design: Julie Snow,
Tyson McElvain, Connie Lindor
Julie Snow Architects
2400 Rand Tower
527 Marquette Avenue
Minneapolis, MN 55402
612/359-9430
www.juliesnowarchitects.com
Produced by Linda O'Keeffe
and Alecia Stevens
Original story written by Alecia Stevens
Photography by John Reed Forsman

90
Architecture: William Hefner
Design: Kazuko Hoshino
William Hefner, Inc.
5820 Wilshire Boulevard, Suite 500
Los Angeles, CA 90036
323/931-1365
www.williamhefner.com
Produced by Laura Hull
Original story written by Susan Morgan
Photography by Grey Crawford

91
Design: Patrizio Fradiani
Studio F Design
4201 N. Ravenswood, No. 103A
Chicago, IL 60613
773/880-0450
www.studiof-design.com
Produced by Elana Frankel
and Lisa Skolnik
Original story written by Raul Barreneche
Photography by Jeff McNamara

92
Architecture/Design: Marek Slosar
Slosar Design
4615 El Centro Avenue
Oakland, CA 94602
510/531-5224
www.slosardesign.com
and
Lucian Rosciszewski
Lucian Design Group, Inc.
405 Davis Court, Suite 2201
San Francisco, CA 94111
415/994-1488
www.luciandesign.com
Produced by Linda O'Keeffe and
Jody Kennedy
Original Story written by Lori Conner
Photography by Shaun Sullivan

93
Architecture: Michael Kim
Michael Kim Associates
1 Holden Street
Brookline MA 02445
617 739 6925
www.mkimarchitecture.com
Design: Frank Roop
Frank Roop Design Interiors
224 Clarendon Street, Suite 31
Boston, MA 02116
617/267-0818
www.frankroop.com
Produced by Elana Frankel
Original story written by Kate Walsh
Photography by Catherine Tighe

94
Design: Christopher Coleman
and Angel Sanchez
Christopher Coleman Interior Design
55 Washington Street, Suite 707
Brooklyn, NY 11201
718/222-8984
www.ccinteriordesign.com
Produced by Linda O'Keeffe
Photography by Annie Schlechter

95
Architecture/Design:
Sir Terence Conran
The Conran Group
22 Shad Thames
London SE1 2YU
+44-207-403-8899
www.conran.co.uk
Original story written by Arlene Hirst
Photography by David Garcia

96
Architeture: Travis L. Price III, FAIA
Travis Price Architects
1028 33rd Street NW, Suite 320
Washington, D.C. 20007
202/965-7000
www.travispricearchitects.com
Produced by Elana Frankel
and Barbara Bohl
Original story written by Michael Lassell
Photography by Catherine Tighe

97
Architecture: Hugh Newell Jacobsen
Jacobsen Architecture
2529 P Street NW
Washington, D.C. 20007
202/337-5200
www.hughjacobsen.com
Produced by Linda O'Keeffe
and Barbara Bohl
Original story written by Fred A. Bernstein
Photography by John Granen

98
Architecture/Design: Dan Friedlander
and Richard Foster
Guthrie Friedlander Architects
290 Townsend Street
San Francisco, CA 94107
415/543-5466
www.limn.com
Produced by Donna Warner
Photography by Grey Crawford
Original story written by Fred A. Bernstein

99
Design: Jill Dupré
J Design Salon
2835 Esplanade Avenue
New Orleans, LA 70119
504/908-3539
www.jdesignsalon.com
Produced by Linda O'Keeffe
and Ellen Johnson
Original story written by Sharon Donovan
Photography by Sara Essex

100
Concept and Design: Maya Lin
Maya Lin Studio
www.mayalin.com
Architecture: David Hotson
David Hotson Architect
176 Grand Street, 2nd floor
New York, NY 10013
212/965-8828
www.hotson.net
Furniture selection:
Alan Tanksley
Alan Tanksley Inc.
186 Fifth Avenue, 2nd Floor
New York, NY 10010
212/481-8454
www.alantanksley.com
Produced by Linda O'Keeffe
Original story written by Fred A. Bernstein
Photography by Antoine Bootz